westland ltd

The Winning Way

Anita is the content person for Prosearch. A post-graduate in Statistics from the Indian Institute of Technology, Mumbai and a post-graduate from the Indian Institute of Management, Ahmedabad, Anita started her career in advertising with stints at Contract and FCB-Ulka. She then spent about ten years running a communication consultancy and qualitative research agency, even scripting and producing three TV ad commercials. The name Prosearch comes from this professional research experience. From 1998 to 2001, Anita went back to FCB-Ulka to head their strategic planning and research department. In 2001, Harsha came on board since sports marketing was coming of age in India and Prosearch saw a big opportunity in the area. Harsha's ringside view of sports combined with Anita's experience with brands and new business pitches helps Prosearch effectively marry sports and management and makes their offering unique to the Indian market.

* * *

Harsha makes the presentations that Anita creates and in doing so, they play to each other's strengths. He has had a most unusual career since graduating in Chemical Engineering from Osmania University, Hyderabad and doing a post-graduate programme from Indian Institute of Management, Ahmedabad.

After working in advertising for two years and in a sports management firm for another two years he moved into the world of broadcasting and has now emerged as the face of Indian cricket and is widely believed to be India's leading sports commentator. For the last twelve years he has presented cricket on ESPN and Star Sports and has even had a talent hunt named after him — *Hunt for Harsha!* His exposure to the world of management not only provides him with different insights into sport and broadcasting but helps marry Anita's strong thinking into a very successful corporate programme.

The Winning Way

by
Anita Bhogle &
Harsha Bhogle

westland

westland ltd
Venkat Towers, 165, P.H. Road, Maduravoyal, Chennai 600 095
No. 38/10 (New No. 5), Raghava Nagar, New Timber Yard Layout, Bangalore 560 026
Survey No. A-9, II Floor, Moula Ali Industrial Area, Moula Ali, Hyderabad 500 040
23/181, Anand Nagar, Nehru Road, Santacruz East, Mumbai 400 055
47, Brij Mohan Road, Daryaganj, New Delhi 110 002

First published by westland ltd 2011

10 9 8 7 6 5 4 3 2 1

ISBN: 978-93-80658-32-2

Inside book formatting and typesetting by Ram Das Lal

Printed at Manipal Press Ltd., Manipal

To our fathers R.S. Kulkarni and A.D. Bhogle
whom we remember every day and who so influenced
us. How we would have loved to present them this.

To our mothers Lily Kulkarni and Shalini Bhogle
in whose lap we first sought, and received, shelter
and who have always been there for us.

Acknowledgements

Long before this book was an idea, and to be honest it remained an idea for a long time, Mukul Deoras (then of Hindustan Unilever and now MD of Colgate Palmolive India) invited us to present at one of their events. 'The Winning Way', as we called the presentation, seemed interesting then and it is just as interesting today, 300 sessions later. So thanks a lot for being the catalyst, Mukul.

Cricket and advertising have been an integral part of our life and those learnings form the basis of a major part of this book. We were helped by the fact that cricketers, and other sportsmen, like Sachin Tendulkar, Virender Sehwag, Ian Chappell, Sanjay Manjrekar, Nasser Hussain and Viren Rasquinha agreed to speak to us. You will find their contributions at various points in this book.

But cricket is half the story. Almost all of the clients who invited us to their events were willing to talk to us about their organisations and the issues they faced. This helped us tailor presentations for them but also helped us draw the links between sport and corporate life better. Many of them, as you would imagine, were sports lovers and that made the dialogue easier. They provided the critical input to this book.

And specifically we asked people to offer insights into management and corporate situations. Inevitably, they said 'yes' and we were moved by how much time they were willing to give us. This is like a who's who of corporate India and they lend the weight to the book it could not otherwise have acquired. So, a big thank you to:

Jaithirth (Jerry) Rao, former Country head, Consumer Banking, Citibank India and founder and former CEO, Mphasis

Nitin Paranjpe, CEO and MD, Hindustan Unilever

Mukul Deoras, MD, Colgate-Palmolive (India) Ltd

Niall S.K. Booker, Chief Executive Officer, HSBC North America Holdings Inc

Subroto Bagchi, Gardener & Vice Chairman, MindTree Ltd

Neeraj Garg, COO, True Care business, Abbott Truecare Pharma Pvt. Ltd

Sandip Das, Group CEO, Maxis Communications Berhad

Saugata Gupta, CEO, Consumer Products Business, Marico Ltd

Sunil Lulla, Managing Director and CEO, Times Television Network

Shailesh Ayyangar, MD, Sanofi-Aventis India and VP, South Asia, Global Operations

Anindo Mukherjee, Managing Director, General Mills India

Madhabi Puri-Buch, MD and CEO, ICICI Securities

Marten Pieters, MD and CEO, Vodafone Essar

Bharat Puri, Senior Vice President, Global Chocolate, Kraft Foods

Deep Kalra, Founder and CEO, MakeMyTrip.com

Vivek Kudva, Managing Director, India and CEEMEA, Franklin Templeton Investments

Tiger Tyagarajan, Chief Operating Officer, Genpact

and our closest friend and sounding board A.S. Ramchander, Regional Marketing Director, Asia and Pacific region, Castrol Lubricants

In our first meeting with Gautam and Paul of Westland we knew we had found our publishers. It is a critical association for each must understand the other and we are very happy with them. They suggested that a young, enthusiastic, cricket lover, Karthik, be the editor. We went by their suggestion and it was a good one. Karthik was quick and had the ability to spot things that might have stuck out. It meant that we had to work a bit more after we thought the book was done but it was a wise decision.

For the last word, for an excellent after mint, we wanted something from a great team player. Among his glittering achievements, and ones that numbers will not show, Rahul Dravid can take pride in being an outstanding competitor and human being. Thank you Rahul, not for the first time and, maybe, not for the last.

And one day while thinking about who we could request to write the foreword, we thought we would be audacious and ask Mukesh Ambani. We have had an association through his wife, Nita; both our children have benefitted from being at her excellent school, and on the few occasions we had met him he had come across as being extremely down to earth and approachable and to our eternal joy, he said yes. We cannot thank him enough.

And so our book has Rahul Dravid and Mukesh Ambani on it. Life must be good.

Contents

Foreword

Sport and business have much in common. Competitiveness, dynamism, uncertainty, strategy and execution, and above all, leadership and team work.

As businesses and corporations take on newer and greater global challenges, they will have to rapidly and efficiently disseminate best practices to their people in a decentralized yet effective manner. Building capacity and speedily bridging competence gaps will have to be done in unique and innovative ways. Anita and Harsha Bhogle attempt such an innovation in a most outstanding way — by drawing out business lessons from sport in a gripping book.

I have loved sport since childhood, especially cricket!

This book took me down memory lane. It brought all my memories of sport and business alive. With the advent of the Indian Premier League (IPL), my wife Nita and I have become more closely associated with cricket. We have ourselves learned a great deal in business from this association.

Harsha has been an integral part of Indian cricket's growth. He is part of an ecosystem which has put India on the global map. Indian cricket is now globally respected and admired — thanks to the important role that Harsha has played in the process.

Harsha has made us romance and understand cricket. His insightful mind has never ceased to amaze me. His immaculate analysis of the game brings new perspectives to one's mind. His personal relationships with great sportsmen have given him unique insights into the game and the minds of its masters. His ability to do parallel processing of information and convert it into golden nuggets, garnished by eloquent language is truly astonishing!

His partnership with Anita is a great example of how two people can work together. Her sharp, incisive mind, honed by many years in the advertising world, is at the heart of the work they do and you can see her touch all along. She is the genuine modern all-rounder and as they advocate in the book, they set up a goal for each other to score.

This book, *The Winning Way*, is a great collation of Anita and Harsha's knowledge of sport.

They have gathered little pearls of wisdom at the intersection of sport, business, cinema and life, which can be found on almost every page of this book.

Reading this book is as pleasurable an experience as listening to a commentary — indeed, more so. The language has a beautiful flow and the writing is replete with appropriate examples and anecdotes. Their trademark touch is remarkably refreshing.

The Winning Way is an invigorating read. Understanding the business world through the lens of sport is stimulating and energizing. The book has expressively and compellingly laid out the 'ground rules' of winning!

This book is a great gift to ambitious aspirants from the corporate as well as the entrepreneurship worlds. I do hope the values and lessons derived get well entrenched in the future global leaders.

March 2011   —*Mukesh D. Ambani*
Mumbai

1

Why This Book?

I believe in an athlete's life, winning is important, but, the journey is more meaningful! The constant pursuit toward overcoming one's own limitations and always challenging the part of you that says you will not or cannot win! I am convinced that everybody has, at some time in their life, faced an equivalent. Something that feels insurmountable. My, perhaps unsolicited, advice is enjoy the ride! Let's face it, roller coasters are far more thrilling than merry go rounds!
—Abhinav Bindra

Eight years ago we started a motivational series called 'The Winning Way'. It is a workshop that draws learnings from sport and applies them to organisations. It talks about what champion sportspeople and winning teams do in all kinds of sport, the practices they follow, the habits they cultivate — and it tries to draw parallels with corporate issues and situations. 'The Winning Way' stems from our deep-rooted belief that the formula for winning remains the same whether you are a sportsman, a musician, a financial planner, a pharmaceutical salesman or a housewife. Since the principles behind success remain the same, anyone using them should be able to reach their full potential and succeed.

Since 'The Winning Way' has received several repeat requests from Microsoft, HSBC, Unilever, Glaxo SmithKline, Aventis, Cadbury's, Marico, Castrol, Colgate and the like, we have felt encouraged enough to put together this book. It consists of our reflections on winning, what constitutes a winner and how all of us can, to put it simply, win.

The past few years have been a continuous learning process for us. We have witnessed up close the rise and fall of several cricket captains, the emergence of Twenty20 as an interesting innovation in the sport, the metamorphosis of Indian cricket under Ganguly and Dhoni and the domination of Australia in all forms of the game. We have seen many sportspersons up close through their ups and downs. While doing all of this, through our workshop we also interacted with stalwarts from industry, many of them passionate followers of sports themselves, and this interaction enriched the dialogue. This book then, while making no claims about being a complete handbook on winning is the collation of our collective learning – from the world of sport and the world of business.

In 2004, along with CNBC, we produced a novel programme called *Masterstrokes* where every episode saw a cricketer and a corporate head discuss various aspects of winning. It reinforced our belief that there was much that managers could learn from sport.

Over the last eight years, we have travelled across countries and cities, speaking about winning and what it takes to win. This book draws from our work spanning close to 300 sessions for 150 companies across almost all sectors. There were old economy companies trying to cope with market changes and simultaneously, with a changed, new generation; there were companies that had issues arising from growth and globalisation; some were reeling under the burden of their own growth and some companies were in businesses so new that they didn't know how different their tomorrow would look from today. The one thread that was common to such diversely-placed businesses was that they all were keen on winning. We also realized as we went along speaking to these supposedly diverse businesses that whatever your product or service may be, in today's world where technology and processes can be outsourced, plant and machinery imported and finance acquired very easily, that it finally boiled down to people. And with these people being drawn from the same common pool, it was only team culture and environment, leadership and vision, attitude towards change and occasional failure that determined how well the team performed.

The years 2008-09 saw the dark cloud of recession hover over the economy, bringing with it salary cuts, pink slips and tremendous insecurity. This was a huge challenge for everyone but especially for new entrants to the corporate world who had come in with dreams of a boom time and for HR managers in sectors like IT and BPOs with a very young employee profile. Senior managers too told us that they needed to hang on to their jobs since there weren't that many for their kind of profile.

As we made this journey, interestingly, we found that winning was not this 'one size fits all' cloak of invincibility. It wasn't a trophy or medal that would look just as good in any display or a rose that would smell just as sweet in any boardroom. Winning came in different shades and sizes The ambitions of companies and their mission statements varied dramatically. The big realisation was that size does matter but that size isn't everything. That you could have goals, and sometimes need to have goals other than being No. One. Also, that the problems that winners have are often bigger and more complicated than those of the also-rans. Over eight years we have seen the business environment changing and along with it we have seen corporate India start to approach success very differently. With many of the companies, we did an exercise where we asked executives to analyse which international cricket team their own team resembled and which one they aspired to be like. In many cases, the first hurdle was for the executives to figure out what exactly was meant by 'teams' as new-age organisational structures, global reporting relationships etc. have given an all new twist to this term. That sorted out, many teams aspired to be Australia, the unquestioned leader. But as India started winning, first under Ganguly and then Dhoni, more and more people rooted for India as the team they wanted to emulate. Interestingly, it was also the time when L.N. Mittal and Ratan Tata made it to the covers of international magazines.

We have often wondered if in recent years the state of the Indian economy and the state of Indian cricket seem to be closely correlated. Is it a mere coincidence that Arcelor and Corus happened around the same time as India's Twenty20 victory in 2007? Would Ganguly and Dhoni be at ease discussing leadership issues with Nandan Nilekani and Sunil Bharti Mittal — on how to motivate a young India with global dreams and an attitude to match? And to think that when we started our careers in 1985, nobody challenged the Levers and the Tatas — quite like Indian cricket was happy with respectable draws against England or the West Indies.

Those pre-liberalisation times were uncomplicated and young executives like us, naïve and simple. Dreams were limited and constraints were more talked about than ambition. Life was simple, media options limited and job security was paramount to most people. There were a few good brands and few aspirational employers. As young advertising professionals, we were account planning, media planning, servicing people all rolled into one. There was no need for specialisation. When we read retail audit reports and noted small changes in brand share, the boss would ask 'Grown by volume or value?' That was our first lesson that winning on paper was one thing. Winning in the marketplace, through actual volume growth something else.

Today, the stakes attached to winning are very high, whether in sport or in business. People see the growth of cricket in

India mostly in financial terms for that has been the most dramatic rise. But the world over, the game itself has evolved by leaps and bounds. The contest between bat and ball is the same, but elements like fitness, speed and strategy have become critical and changed the face of the game beyond recognition. New variants of the game like Twenty20 too have emerged. With corporate entry into franchises, the game has become even more exciting and challenging.

We are therefore in a strange situation today. On the one hand, it's a 'perform or perish' kind of pressure situation. On the other hand, leaders are also constantly being told to nurture and empower their teams, understand the whole person rather than merely assess the young man or woman at the workplace. So, can the hand that cracks the whip also be the reassuring hand on an over burdened shoulder? Winning today is about finding the balance between being encouraging and being ruthless. Unlike in other areas, winning in sport gives a high not only to those who play but also to people like us who follow it. It's a high that is cherished and talked about long after the event. There are few things in life more inspiring and motivating than sport. This book attempts to share some insights on winning through examples from the fascinating world of real-life champions.

2

The Business of Winning

An athlete cannot run with money in his pockets. He must run with hope in his heart and dreams in his head.

—Emil Zatopek

Television, sport's greatest ally, creates dramatic images of adrenalin-fuelled athletes making a courageous, even frantic, rush towards victory. There are few sights more moving than victory or brave defeat or indeed heroic effort. Remember Sachin Tendulkar braving the sandstorm and the opposition at Sharjah in 1998, or Anil Kumble bowling with a broken jaw in Antigua in 2002, or Misbah-ul-huq down on the ground after having tried so hard in the first World Twenty20 championship in 2007? But winning and losing are no more than the last step in a much longer journey; a crucial step, but just one step. Teams that journey better take that last step better, far more easily. Teams that flounder and lose their way in between may reach the end, but in all likelihood, with someone ahead of them.

So why do some teams win more often than others? Why are some teams more mercurial, capable of astonishing performances one day and appalling ones the next? Is there a formula to winning that only some possess? Or is it out there for everybody to follow but only some are inclined to reach out for it? Is there a culture to winning, then? And if there is, why do some teams embrace it with passion while others merely look at it from a distance?

The Winning Cycle

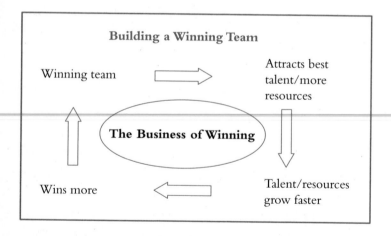

The ideal situation for teams would be to search for that often elusive cycle of winning. The good news is that it exists; maybe more like Boyle's Law maybe, with conditions attached, than like the basic laws of mathematics that are rigid and therefore, more universal! And many teams around the world seem able to create such a cycle and keep it going.

Good players like playing in winning teams and as teams create an aura around themselves, youngsters dream of being part of the legacy. Inevitably therefore, winning teams attract the best talent and because they create a climate where talent is allowed to flourish, players get better faster and that contributes to winning more often. Manchester United, Real Madrid and the Los Angeles Lakers, for example, seem to have created that cycle. Australia's cricket team seem able to do it. And when we were passing out of IIM-A in the mid-Eighties, Hindustan Lever had a similar aura. The best graduates went there, they learnt faster and it became a breeding ground for new corporate leaders. As a result, a day into the placement season we looked at the guys who had made it there with a mixture of awe and confusion. They were one of us but suddenly seemed to be a couple of inches taller!

When asked what creates this aura, Nitin Paranjpe, MD and CEO, Hindustan Unilever Limited elaborated, 'First and foremost is the capacity to demonstrate that you can win consistently. But that is not enough. You could win and still not have the aura. And that is because of how you go about it. One aspect of that is the means you use to win, the values you demonstrate. The second aspect is how you are seen by others — whether you are a thought leader, whether you have a clear point of view about the future well before the others.

The success that you thus achieve feeds on itself. But winning today is not enough. You need to win today and tomorrow.'[1]

* * *

In corporate India where movement is much freer than it is in predominantly inter-country sport, companies seek to be employers of choice almost as much they seek market share. They know that if you create the right environment, talent will flourish. Organisations rarely have to tell talented, driven players to perform. More often, they just need to make them feel good. Sourav Ganguly would never have had to go to Sachin Tendulkar and say, 'Sachin, please, we need a fifty from you. The team really needs it!' Tendulkar probably wants to score that fifty, or hundred, more than anyone else but if the atmosphere in the dressing room is not conducive, his mind is likely to be full of negative thoughts, as indeed it can be in organisations that employ ambitious men and women. When companies start becoming completely goal-centric and forget that it is people who produce results, they struggle. Just as players in good teams enjoy going to compete, so should people going to work; only one reason why the human resource function is such an important aspect of winning teams! Human resource management becomes even more important during tough times, prompting N.R. Narayana Murthy to remark, 'At Infosys we say at 9.00 am when every one of our people is working, the marketcap may be whatever it is, 15 or 16 in these tough days, but at 6.15 or 7.00 pm or maybe 9.00 pm, when the last of us has gone home, the marketcap is zero.'[2]

In his wonderful book, *The Winner Within*, the former coach of the Los Angeles Lakers, Pat Riley, writes of the great bonding in the team that helped in winning the NBA title in 1980. But towards the end of the season a young man called Magic Johnson, soon to take the world by storm, came off the substitute bench and played a leadership role. At the start of the next season the team got drawn into the rivalry, partially media created, between Johnson and the erstwhile star Kareem Abdul Jabbar. A battle of one-upmanship can be good in a team upto a stage since the points a player scores contribute to the team score anyway. But beyond a point, the objective can be to outdo one another rather than do what is best for the team and that can be disastrous for morale and results. The Lakers, now a team in disarray, made one of the fastest exits a defending champion has made going out in the first round of the playoffs in 1981. Two match-winners had collided and taken the team down with them when a harmonious environment might have had the two champions standing shoulder-to-shoulder.

What Causes Winning Cycles to Break

Often discord can be produced by players who put individual goals ahead of the team interest. They are not too difficult to spot. The forward who looks for the dramatic goal from an impossible angle rather than slide it to an unmarked teammate; the batsman who slows down in quest of a hundred in a one-day international and ends up costing his team an extra twenty runs; the publicity-seeking boss who claims credit for a great product launch... It is vital that players, medical reps, real-estate sales executives, anyone really, have personal goals otherwise we would be robots without them. There are times however, when teams get into trouble when a collection of such strictly individual goals derails the team ethic.

So as you can see, winning cycles can break if there is discord, or if young blood, instead of competing, stays on the bench for too long. If there is no room for fresh talent, teams can stagnate, in performance and in thought. Players need to be challenged all the time, it is what keeps them hungry and excited, and like nature, organisations must have mechanisms not only for nurturing but also culling. Australia remained strong because they had a very rigourous, almost brutal, exit policy. When Ian Healy wanted to finish in front of his home crowd, he was told he couldn't because Adam Gilchrist was ready. Steve Waugh wanted to finish his career with a win in India in 2004 but was told he wasn't going to stay that long. And at the first sign of decline in Gilchrist, the word must have gone out too. At Manchester United when Wayne Rooney and Cristiano Ronaldo arrived, Ruud van Nistelroy was bid goodbye and Ryan Giggs was found more often on the bench than in the field. When young players realize they are getting an opportunity because of a stringent exit policy, they also know that they can't linger when their time comes.

Too often teams spend time retaining talent, whereas culling it when the time comes is a ruthless, but just as necessary, way of keeping a winning cycle going. Instead, when teams dither, hanging on to players because of sentiment or as a reward, they run the risk of getting stuck with a lot of players on the declining side of a product life cycle curve and end up losing a lot of players simultaneously. Also, the message going out to the younger replacements is that the individual matters more than the team. That is where Australia have been good over the years; nurturing their players and backing them to the hilt while, at the same time, recognising the need to create hungry teams. In contrast, the general feeling was that Jayasuriya and Kapil Dev were allowed to hang around a bit longer than was necessary.

A steady inflow of fresh and young talent becomes potent only when that talent is encouraged to think and empowered to express their views. McKinsey makes it obligatory for its young managers to 'agree to disagree'. Getting people to express their views leads to greater accountability. Once a decision is taken and the whole team comes on board, it is difficult to pass the buck. Bharat Puri, former MD of Cadbury India Ltd believes that great communication is a hallmark of winning teams and that depends on whether it is the organisation's culture to promote open communication.[3]

There might be shifts in technology or demographics or government policy as well that could cause winning cycles to break. Great Test teams could look out of place in a Twenty20 environment for example. Players born into an atmosphere of not letting a bowler get them out discovered that they had to play with a different set of values; that being out after belting a quick 30 was more valuable than denying a bowler a wicket and making 35 in 60 balls. In such a situation, teams can look dated and in desperate need of newer players with more contemporary skills. At other times, you may need to change coaches, or for that matter consultants, who might be stuck in a time capsule. When Twenty20 cricket first arrived the players hadn't played it but coaches hadn't experienced it either. So their traditional role, which was to impart knowledge based on their own experience, was under threat. To give a slightly different example, when hockey went the astro-turf way, with hard hitting and quick movements, India's coaches were still stuck on grass, trying to play a beautiful, dribbling and skills-oriented but obsolete game!

So as we have seen, teams need to cull with the same intensity with which they need to nurture. The best teams are those that back their players all the way but when they find that players can no longer contribute for various reasons, becoming irrelevant is but one of those, they don't waste time in letting them go.

Iconic brands, otherwise, might end up becoming 'dad's brands' and we saw that when India's economy was opened us and became market driven, companies that had thrived on licenses and monopolies and didn't really care about the customer, virtually perished. For a long time the Indian two-wheeler market was dominated by the scooter and when we were young, bikes were for the somewhat reckless, wannabe young men. Scooters had stepneys in case you got a flat, while bikers didn't care too much about these things. But the scooter was a solid middle-class possession and Bajaj was the god who could deliver one to you. Waitlists stretched for ten years and so Bajaj really didn't need to compete with anybody. Then Hero Honda soon started a revolution — riding a scooter became terribly passé, you didn't get flat tyres anymore and Bajaj was forced to compete. The iconic Rahul Bajaj gave way to a younger generation who manufactured motorcycles which competed admirably with Hero Honda. Bajaj culled in time or else they could have ended up with the equivalent of classy Test players in a Twenty20 team.

While Bajaj was able to re-establish the cycle, leading camera companies were unable to prevent the advance of the cell phone that took photographs. A dramatic change in technology broke the winning cycle for them as it did for Australia in the early years of Twenty20 cricket.

Apart from such major changes there are others than can cause a winning cycle to break. Teams can at times take their foot off the pedal, lose the focus on winning and let faults build up (while they are winning) until they become critical and almost impossible to conceal. Some people believe that Colgate-Palmolive fell into this trap in the late Nineties when they let Hindustan Lever outflank them for a while with the launch of the Pepsodent and Close-Up brands which were targeted specifically at the youth. As it turned out it was just the wake-up call Colgate needed to return strongly. Indeed, in the early days of their long association, Colgate-Palmolive's brief to their advertising agency, Rediffusion was 'Don't change anything'. One got the impression that Colgate-Palmolive didn't exactly know which part of their winning formula was working and so didn't want to change anything for fear of removing the successful elements.

Sometimes good teams can take winning for granted, delude themselves into thinking they merely need to turn up to win; they let the arrogance remain but let the work ethic dwindle. There was always a suspicion that this was the case with the teams that followed the great West Indies outfits of the late Seventies, Eighties and early Nineties; the arrogance remained, the work ethic vanished! To prevent teams from starting to think that they have, in a sense 'arrived', Deep Kalra, founder and CEO, MakeMyTrip.com, suggests that one think of success as a moving target. As he puts it, 'The trick is tell yourself every day that all this "success" business is firstly relative … it helps to look at companies(in his case) like Apple, Facebook, Google and Amazon, or the entrepreneurs behind them and secondly, success is mercurial … it can go as soon as it comes. especially once you have public market stock.'[4]

But let us return to winning. Probably the biggest reason some teams win more often than others is that they know how to win. Many years ago, Michel Platini, one of the finest football players in the world, said the team that would win the soccer World Cup would be the team that knew how to. You might scoff at this simplistic statement. But if you examine it closely you'll probably come around to the conclusion that there is a lot of truth in it.

Why Some Teams Can't Keep the Winning Cycle Going

Teams that don't win very often, inevitably don't know what to do when placed in a winning position. They freeze. They choke. As do teams that are so obsessed with the idea of winning that they grow tense and often stop thinking when a calm mind would have taken them home. Maybe there is a story then behind South Africa's misadventures in the World Cup. After a dramatic re-entry to international cricket in 1992, they often found themselves in winning positions and threw it away; never more obvious than in the dramatic 1999 World Cup semi-final when they had tied the scores and needed only a single from four balls. First Allan Donald charged out for a non-existent single and almost ran himself out and then Lance Klusener, who was hitting the ball wherever he wanted to, hit the ball and ran. Donald didn't. The two players froze, with victory waiting at their doorstep.

The fear of winning can sometimes be greater than the fear of losing! That is why winning a Test series against Australia in 2008 was seen by South Africans as being as important as winning the rugby World Cup on a dramatic night in 1995; the beast, which for so long was an annoying tenant, was finally off their back. Yet, when it came to cricket World Cup events, the tenant inevitably reappeared. For a team with an outstanding win percentage in bilateral series, they continued to choke in mega world events. As a consequence, their obsession with getting results at times derailed the performance that could get them there in the first place.

A young player growing up in that otherwise excellent South African side would have inherited the tension associated with winning on a big day. On the other hand, a young man learning his trade in Australia's awesome teams through the mid-Nineties and the first decade of the new millennium, would have seen how senior players were focused on winning. A young man like Michael Clarke, sharing the dressing room with the likes of Shane Warne, Glenn McGrath, Ricky Ponting, Mathew Hayden and Adam Gilchrist would have learnt how to win, how to close matches as part of his upbringing in international cricket. An equally talented young man like Mohd. Ashraful of Bangladesh, growing up in a losing environment, could never have learnt the discipline of winning. Self-belief is an essential aspect of development and if you are not winning, you'll never acquire it. We are sure our friends in Hindustan Lever, many of whom have gone on to have outstanding careers, will have a similar story of learning to tell. As indeed will companies that failed to close deals; either because they thought they already had them in the bag, or because they didn't quite know what to do at that crucial last stage.

In 2006, Australia went to Bangladesh at the end of a very long and tiring season. The players were exhausted (Brett Lee famously said there was no fuel in the tank, only fumes), they wanted to be home and it seemed a rare occasion to see an Australian team wanting to put its feet up rather than play cricket. They were not as intense as they normally were and maybe took things for granted (Another vital truth about sport and live television is that if you take things for granted it can be quite unforgiving.) At the end of the first day, Bangladesh were 355 for 5, a situation that was entirely unexpected and one they had scarcely found themselves in before. To our astonishment, their captain Habibul Bashar said at the press conference later in the evening that if they scored another hundred runs they would be 'safe'. We were astounded but you can understand where Bashar was coming from. If, all your life, you have aspired not to lose, being 'safe' is an accomplishment.

The next day they had Australia down at 145 for 6 and Adam Gilchrist was at the press conference. 'We're in a bit of a hole, and need to figure out how to win from here,' he said and in that moment, you could see the difference between the two sides. The underdogs, through years of defeat, were unaware that they were in a winning position. Opportunity had knocked on their door, they didn't recognize it. They weren't ready for it. The champions, an the other hand were always moving ahead, they were focussing on victory. It came as no surprise when Australia won, despite the fact that they had defeat staring them in the face on more than one occasion during the course of the match. Bangladesh were left thinking whether it could have been a turning point in their cricketing history! Which is why it is often said that to be a champion, you need big match temperament.

You'll find too that organisations that can't quite 'close matches' spend the rest of their lives wondering what might have been and getting frustrated when they find that the world doesn't really have time for their kind. Quite apart from this example, you'll find that good teams are able to put the past behind them and focus on the present; to accept the situation as given and not grieve over what might have been. A couple of youngsters in the Rajasthan Royals team that won the first IPL said their captain Shane Warne was always telling them, 'How can we win from here?' Sachin Tendulkar is like that, and so was Anil Kumble — always trying to look ahead rather than worrying about why they got into a bad situation in the first place.

It's a peculiar paradox. To know how to win, you must win frequently as Aristotle once said, 'We are what we repeatedly do. Excellence then is not an act, but a habit'. You cannot be lackadaisical all your life and suddenly seek discipline in the middle of a big innings or before a big game. If you are a company that has always cut costs you cannot suddenly decide to become a big advertising spender. If you have grown up in a family with few means at its disposal, you will still eat the last corner slice of bread or vigorously shake the bottle of ketchup to extract the last drop even if you can easily afford another one. If you are a family-driven company, you cannot suddenly become a professionally-managed company, as Kumaramangalam Birla discovered when, as a young man, he took over the companies his charismatic father Aditya Birla had managed.

Winners Take Away Hope from the Oppositon

Teams that win therefore, and win consistently, begin acquiring an aura around them. People write about them, opponents read that and watch in awe and when the time comes to compete, their rivals lack the self-belief so vital to a good contest. Losing becomes a self-fulfilling prophecy. This is one of the great truths in sport and that is why a lot of matches are won and lost before the match begins. Great teams are aware of this and that is why Australia's stated objective before the World Cup of 2003 was to create awe in the opposing dressing room. It meant that Australia would play and produce results in a manner that would allow them to focus on their game while forcing their opponents to concentrate not on their own game, as they should have, but instead on Australia.

Similar instances have taken place in the past — when the West Indies were virtually invincible through the late Seventies and mid-Eighties, opponents would look at a line up that read Greenidge, Haynes, Richards, Richardson, Gomes, Lloyd, Dujon, Marshall, Roberts, Holding and Garner. It created a sense of hopelessness in them and opposing teams have often spoken of losing matches before they had started. It's an interesting phenomenon this: creating hopelessness. The strongest weapon a team has on the field is hope. Till such time as hope is alive, they believe that they can win. Once hope dies, the end is swift. Steve Waugh, who was part of Australian teams that lost to the West Indies, often spoke of the desire to reach a similar level; where his team could win matches before they even began. Can organisations, like the West Indies cricket team, or indeed the great Bombay Ranji Trophy teams, kill hope before a contest starts? In her Harry Potter series, J.K. Rowling writes about the prison at Azkaban where soulless creatures called Dementors suck hope and happiness from the prisoners. These aren't torture chambers, no Guantanamo Bay here, they merely suck hope and that is why Azkaban was such a terrifying place.

It is an interesting exercise for organisations to carry out. Does your team have hope? Even on an off day, or after a poor quarter, does the team believe it can win? If the opposite is true, the leader has a job on hand; not necessarily to win the game but to instill belief in his team that could lead to a win.

This 'hopelessness' was vividly demonstrated before the semi-final of the Ranji Trophy in April 1991. The evening before the match, in the course of an informal discussion, it was suggested that Hyderabad had a chance against mighty Bombay, as they were then called. One of the players seemed to disagree. 'Nonsense,' he said (and here we are attempting a translation from the more colourful Hyderabadi dialect) 'if you get the openers out, Manjrekar walks in, if you get him out, Tendulkar comes in, then Vengsarkar, then Kambli, then Pandit, how many do you think we can dismiss?' Bombay batted the next day and went on to declare at 855-6 scored at just under 5 an over. A match had been lost even before it had begun and the action on the field was merely a self-fulfilling prophecy at work. Indeed at one stage when the Hyderabad captain pulled up a fielder for letting a boundary go through he was told, 'What difference does four runs make when they have made seven hundred!'

To create this sense of hopelessness in the opposition, the Australians decided they would seek to win, not only every Test, but also every day and every session. When the opposition analysed a game, and broke it down session by session, they had to come to the conclusion that they had won very little, if indeed they had won anything at all. And to drive home the point the Aussies made a chart with the days on one axis and sessions on the other. It meant you had fifteen boxes and you ticked a box if you won, put a cross if you lost and an equal sign if the session was squared. Having done so, and discovered that their opponents had very little to show, they actually put the sign outside the dressing room, not inside, so that it could be seen by everyone! While that might have been rubbing it in a bit, the idea behind it was sound. If you want to create an aura you do not allow the opposition to believe they have a chance. If they win a session, they might start believing they could win a day and thereafter a game. They could enter a contest armed with hope and belief. And so it was paramount that every session was conquered for the opposition to feel totally devoid of hope.

Nitin Paranjpe offers an interesting parallel from the world of consumer marketing. 'We have broken down our market into 153 cells,' he says 'and each cell is looked at independently. We might be winning overall but if even 25 of those cells are in red, it is not acceptable. And so while achieving the macro target is the desired outcome, the management of the business has to be more granular.'[5] In effect, HUL aim to win every session, every day, not just every match.

The hopelessness that such domination can generate can be seen through statements the opposition make. After another one-sided Ranji Trophy final the captain of the losing side said, 'It was a privilege for us to play against Sachin Tendulkar,' much in the manner of India's bowlers who were in love with the idea of merely bowling to Don Bradman on their first tour there in 1948. If you are excited just by being on the same stage, chances are you are unlikely to out-perform the opposition.

Teams like these, that can dominate, are often excellent at converting their plans into action. And inevitably, they do the small things better than the opposition can, or wants to. It is incredible how many matches are won by teams that do the simple things, the one per cent things, better. In cricket that means working hard on fitness, running well between wickets, converting the opposition's three runs into two and your own two runs into three, taking catches, throwing at the stumps directly…essentially things that do not require an extraordinary level of playing skill, but which can be learnt by consistent practice. These are teams that can do the difficult things, batting on bad pitches, bowling wicked out-swingers, turning the ball twelve inches on a flat surface very well but assign just as much importance to the one per cent things. It is these one per cent things that produce consistency and you will find that across all areas of industry. Organisations that are consistently successful have strong systems and a framework to enforce those systems. And so in the course of our corporate sessions we often ask people, and the larger teams they represent, what their one per cent things are and how much time they spend practicing working on them. Doing the one per cent things is a sign of humility, while on the other hand ignoring them would be a mark of arrogance. It is also a great indicator of work ethic, the one factor more than any other, that contributes to winning consistently.

'The one per cent things tend to be stuff that is not particularly sexy,' says Niall Booker, Former CEO of HSBC in India, 'and while it's tough to make an improvement of 25 per cent, it's possible to do 25 one-per-centers.' 'In financial services, things like the industrialization of processes, control over data security, the handling of customer complaints and the protocols around the development of talent are the one per cent components. In banking, it could be risk management but more generally, these could be small details like sending thank-you notes to people who have done a good job, sharing a joke with your staff or addressing complaints of your smallest clients and showing them that you care — things that not everybody takes the time to do.'[6]

Mukul Deoras, MD of Colgate-Palmolive (India) Ltd thinks the one per cent is alignment. 'It's not enough to have strategy. Execution is more important and in order to execute, the most important thing is alignment.'[7] Neeraj Garg, COO, Truecare Business, Abbott Truecare Pharma Pvt. Ltd too echoes Mukul's views. 'Sometimes marketing programmes are planned and announced in a big way but marketing collaterals don't reach locations on time. Our different teams plan wonderfully in isolation but the field force that has to execute all this is overloaded because no one has looked at the programmes from his point of view.'[8] You may have thought through 'the big idea' thoroughly, but by overlooking the crucial one per cent you could prevent the idea from being fully effective.

Newsweek magazine once did a great cover story on Tiger Woods and how he dominated his sport. But the biggest revelation about the article was what other leading sports-persons had to say. In that story, Joe Montana, a US pro-football legend said, 'He gets on a roll, and everybody else starts looking at the board to see what Tiger is doing. They are watching TV too, and they should be playing.' That is what champions do. They force you to divert attention from your game to theirs. You don't look at your strengths, you look at theirs! Sometimes you can see this feeling of awe in our markets as well. It used to be said about Hindustan Unilever Limited — that in their hey-day, when they introduced a new product in the market they made life virtually impossible for the opposition. Anindo Mukherjee, Managing Director, General Mills India, formerly with HUL told us, 'In the mid-Eighties, Hindustan Unilever developed a unique technology for soap-making that gave them a huge cost advantage over competitors. Consequently, over the next decade, it became very difficult for other players in this category to compete with them. Several of them fell by the wayside including large, established companies like TOMCO, which was ultimately acquired by HLL. Over this period, Lever's market share rose from the mid-forties to mid-Seventies. For competitors, it was a hopeless, futile fight.'[9]

Later we were to see something similar with Reliance, a company that intimidated people with the sheer magnitude of their imagination and the ability to convert that into reality. It is a powerful thought and should serve as an inspiration to champions. Ask youself, can you win a match before it begins?

The Look of a Winner

Inevitably then, champions make their intentions known in the manner in which they carry themselves. The key question to ask yourself about a player, or indeed a speaker or a sales executive, is: does he look like he wants to be there? Or does he look like he would rather be elsewhere? When you saw Viv Richards taking the field, you could almost sense the intensity. The swagger as he walked, eyes a bit bloodshot, a few pearls of sweat. He looked more like a heavyweight boxer taking the ring and everything about his body language said, 'Right, I'm here, let's see if you can get me.'

Body language is critical in sport as it is in everything we do because the way we carry ourselves tells the person in front of us what we think about ourselves. As you walk into a situation, your self-image walks along with you as well. You can carry a swagger, you can put on an act for a while but in the end your inner confidence, or lack of it always reveals itself. Dean Jones told us this great story about playing against the West Indies in their glory days. He was a young man and very nervous but was trying to mask it by putting on a brave front. While he was batting, Desmond Haynes at short leg kept laughing. 'What are you laughing about?' Jones asked. 'You're scared, aren't you?' Haynes said. Jones thought he would be a bit smart and said, 'Yeah, but don't tell Joel (Garner).' To which Haynes responded with more laughter. 'What now?' Jones asked. Haynes paused for a moment and replied, 'He already knows,' and broke into more peals of laughter.

Geoffrey Boycott, for example, liked to walk out to bat as soon as the opposition had walked out, to convey to them that he was ready for them, that he was waiting to take them on. Sunil Gavaskar used to get very upset if the two openers didn't walk out together because he thought they were conveying a message to the opposition. And famously, in a Test in the West Indies, when he was hit on the side of the head, he did not even touch the spot — he didn't want the bowler to know that he was hurt. Mohinder Amarnath who was batting at the other end, said he feared for Gavaskar when he heard the sound of the ball hitting him but was amazed when Gavaskar simply stretched himself and got ready for the next delivery. At the end of the over when the substitute, Kiran More, charged out with a glass of water asking if he needed help, he got a earful from Gavaskar. He didn't want to give the bowlers an inch, didn't want to let them know they had scored a point.

Even Tendulkar, known for his great equanimity, has been known to make a point through his body language. 'In my case there have been occasions when the bowlers have said a lot of things and I have not reacted at all. And sometimes I have started it, when I felt that if I do something the bowler might get disturbed and do something else. You don't always need to say something, it might just be looking a bowler in the eye because when you do that the bowler knows you mean business.'

Organisations too have a certain body language as well. For example, Reliance is big, brash, and its scale of operations is mind boggling; the Tatas are firm, understated, classy; Infosys honest and open. It is a good exercise to carry out. Anil Ambani's entertainment venture is called Reliance Big; Infosys came clean when one of their senior managers was accused of sexual harassment; Ratan Tata put his cards on the table and bid goodbye to Singur at some cost to his Nano project. You don't expect Mukesh Ambani to think small either and his ambition of building the world's largest refinery has not surprised anyone.

Probably body language is best manifest in the area of sales where the retailer knows that the salesperson requires the sale to achieve his targets, and yet the salesperson needs to appear committed enough to convince the retailer that it is in his interest to place an order. Sometimes the salesperson, like the leg spinner, needs to sell a couple of extras to the retailer; or the product manager has to appear more convinced than he really is to the advertising agency. It is a game that is critical for success. It is a game that must be played well, not an act that is lightly worn for it can expose people.

Here are some questions every organisation must look at very closely. How do their employees appear to the outside world? What is the message they are subliminally conveying about themselves and their company?

The Winner's Mind

For all their ruthlessness, sportsmen, and indeed all winners need to have the demeanour of a monk. Sport is about calm minds and violent bodies, the reverse rarely works. And yet it is difficult to stay calm amidst the pressure to perform. Abhinav Bindra, India's gold medalist in shooting at the 2008 Beijing Olympics actually practiced it through an unusual combination.

'Essentially, it was adrenaline training — rope-climbing, scaling walls, walking on a tightrope 70 or 80 feet above the ground. The idea is to get a rush, a flow of adrenaline, and then to remain calm in that situation.'[10]

Buddhist monks frequently talk about living in the present and ridding the mind of baggage of the past and the anxiety of the future. Like individual sportsmen, teams tend to carry their baggage with them as well. Teams that have had glorious pasts, like the Indian hockey squad or the Mumbai Ranji

Trophy side can sometimes run the risk of living in the past. We recently met the head of a leading advertising agency who said his company's showreel still began with advertising created in the early Eighties. For years Mumbai cricketers used to talk of their 'glorious heritage' and of how it was easier to play for India than it was to play for Mumbai. Indian coaches, locked in the past focused on dribbling skills unaware that hockey had long transformed into a game of speed and power. Sometimes a great past can make teams oblivious to the present and force them to live in denial. It can frustrate the modern player since he is constantly being compared to legendary figures from the past. A sportsperson succinctly summed it us when he remarked that players seem to get better every day after they retire. Teams need to build on their heritage not get blinded by it and maybe the best way to do it is to embrace the present and address present needs. In fact, Viren Rasquinha, former captain of the Indian hockey team said he couldn't relate to some of his coaches because they talked about players and styles he had never seen.

It is critical that the team on the field is given the impression that it is the lineup of the day; that it is the team that is going to deliver and it must be empowered. Glorifying players who have retired or are unavailable demeans those who are actually playing.

Some other teams might have had a very ordinary past and can carry wounds of defeat. Since the only thing they are good at is losing, they tend to lapse into a cycle of defeat from time to time; often they hold back, taking tentative steps when a giant stride might have made a difference. Teams that are locked into the past need fresh leadership and newer players who have not yet been painted by the brush of defeat. South Africa did that when they picked a brash 22-year-old to be their cricket captain. Graeme Smith had played very little international cricket and was clearly ambitious but his biggest qualification was that he had never played with or under the charismatic, and later disgraced, Hansie Cronje. South Africa needed to turn over a new leaf, break its links with a past that was overwhelming but negative. Initially, there was a great deal of turmoil and pain but it turned out to be an excellent decision.

Good teams are able to leave this baggage behind when they take the field but equally, they are able to put aside the anxiety of the future. Mukul Deoras shares one of the rules that his company followed during the launch of a new product which already had a powerful competitor. 'Be nimble and flexible,' he says, 'to change resources but never lose hope and most importantly, do not demoralize the team, don't make the competitor into an invincible demon.' Winners visualize the rewards of success, losers visualize the penalties of failure.

When asked about why an outstanding Pakistan team lost the final of the 1999 World Cup rather tamely, their captain at the time, the great Wasim Akram, said too many people were worried about what would happened if they lost. And so rather than thinking of winning, they were consumed by the fear of a possible reaction to defeat. It is a telling insight.

Perhaps top sportsmen and teams, top executives and corporations can learn from those Buddhist monks who have a wonderful way of being at peace and living in the present.

Former English cricketer and brilliant coach Bob Woolmer, who died suddenly during the 2007 World Cup, often used to quote Joan Rivers: yesterday is history, tomorrow is a mystery. Good teams win, move on and get ready for the next day.

Symptoms of Winning Teams

- Band of boys atmosphere, happy and relaxed
- Ability to pass the ball
- Living in the present, planning for the future
- Carrying everyone along — backing up underperformers
- A 'can do' approach
- Being attentive to the one per cent things
- Common shared vision
- Strong personal goals yet subordinate to team goals
- Focusing on competition, not internal differences
- Non-negotiable work ethic
- Bringing in new people, ideas to prevent staleness
- Nurturing or culling at the right moment
- Hunger, passion, energy

3

Goals

There's nothing wrong with having your goals really high and trying to achieve them. That's the fun part. You may come up short. I've come up short on a lot on my goals, but it's always fun to try and achieve them.

—Tiger Woods

There are certain things in life that you want to accomplish or milestones that you may wish to achieve — fix a deadline and just go ahead and do them. Then there are others — those wonderful feel good things that you always wanted to do — store them away at the back of your mind for retrieval when you really have the time for them. Occasionally, these thoughts will surface to become interesting topics of conversation and retreat to the inner recesses of your mind soon after. The first set of thoughts or ideas are your goals, the second, your dreams. The moment you put a deadline on your dream, it becomes a goal. And then sometimes it doesn't remain as attractive as it did when it was first stored snugly in your head.

You are accountable for your goals, but not for your dreams and maybe it is the fear of being accountable that keeps some things in the realm of dreamland. For example, thinking, 'I am going to learn how to bowl the slower ball' or 'I am going to send in this beautiful cross from the left' or 'I am going to clean up the house' will remain dreams unless you decide by when you are going to achieve them. There have been many young batsmen who have probably told themselves that they would learn to play the short ball and of course never did; similarly there are many young executives whose to-do list has remained the same on the first of every month.

Goals Must be Out of Reach but Not Out of Sight

So what kind of goals should we set for ourselves so that they are transferred from the realm of fantasy and begin to nudge the real world with a deadline? Perhaps not too high, since that could mean that they will always remain dreams, but not too low either so that achieving them presents no challenge. The classic line of course, and a great line as well, is that goals should be slightly out of reach but never out of sight. One person who did that extraordinarily well all his life was Rahul Dravid, who combined work ethic with great ability. He believes it is always better to set challenging goals even if that means occasionally falling slightly short, rather than set simple goals which could lead to dissatisfaction and leave you wondering if they were too easy. Often people are inclined to set rather simple goals for themselves, and in the process they forget that the kind of goals one sets tells the world what kind of person you are. This is perhaps best highlighted in *Harry Potter and the Chamber of Secrets* when Dumbledore tells the young Harry Potter, 'It is our choices, Harry, that show what we truly are, far more than our abilities.' This applies to young students, sales executives, opening batsmen and leaders of giant corporations equally.

Dravid, like Anil Kumble, is a great example of someone who became as good as he could be. And he did that through a process of setting goals and working diligently towards achieving them. Dravid says that at various points in time he has set performance as well as result goals for himself but believes that performance goals work better for him because the result is not always in his control. 'Even if I set a result goal of scoring a century I could get out to a bad decision or a really good ball or maybe score 95, which still means I haven't reached my goal. Performance goals are far more realistic, achievable and often take the stress out of the result. Besides, if you consistently achieve performance goals, you invariably end up achieving your result goal.' In 1997-98 as he was struggling to find gaps in the field against Kenya and Bangladesh, it seemed he would never be able to become a quality one-day player. Within five years Dravid was India's best finisher, not just the sheet anchor laying the stage for the others but the finisher in limited-overs cricket. In effect when he says it is better to set higher goals, he is talking of what the corporate world calls stretch goals; goals that cause you to dig deeper, extract just that little bit more out of yourself;

cause you to liberate yourself from the comfort zone you are happily ensconced in.

One of the things we do when we have slightly longer sessions with corporate teams is either to analyse case studies or, sometimes, to play a little game like this one: We divide the people into two teams and ask one team to run towards pre-determined spots where a set of tennis balls are kept. Each runner has to reach the spot pick up the ball, throw it to the person collecting it and run towards the next one and so on. There are a couple of rules, one of which is that you cannot throw a ball unless the earlier one has been collected and placed in a basket. The opposing team is allowed to distract you by directing you towards the wrong spot, which can become confusing because it takes time to figure out the order in which you have to run. In one of our sessions we had set 45 seconds as the time in which to carry out the entire sequence of running towards a ball, throwing it to the gatherer, running to the next spot and repeating this exercise over five spots. The first time the sales executives did it, they took between 43 and 47 seconds. We then reset the target to 35 seconds and discovered, maybe because of the learning curve, that most teams could get there as well. At which point, the managing director of the company threw them a challenge. 'Let's show we can do it in 25,' he said and we discovered to our great joy that while nobody could hit 25 seconds, many of them were no more than a couple of seconds away. It was a very simple yet practical demonstration of what Dravid was talking about — that if you set your goals high, you may not always achieve them but you are likely to do much better than when you set small, easily achievable goals. In the session that afternoon, the idea of setting stretch goals went through quite easily.

You Never Know How *Good* You Can Be

Neeraj Garg has an interesting, though slightly different, point of view on this. 'Initially the goal may sound crazy, even unachievable. Then, once you do it, the self-belief is unbelievable. When I was a Area Sales Manager in Karnataka with Hindustan Lever, selling Brooke Bond Red Label Tea, the weekly turnover in a market was 30 tonnes, I announced a week where we would aim to touch 100 tonnes. All our resources were pooled and the target was achieved. This created a "can do" feeling in the team. The subsequent months showed sales settling down at a level lower than 100 but much higher than 30. What you achieve is a function of what you think you can.'[1]

Sadly we do not always know what similar stretch goals are because it is a very rare person who knows how good he or she can be. Imran Khan, one of the all-time greats of the game and an outstanding leader, often talks of how he tried to be the best fast bowler from Pakistan. When he set the goal, he was very far away from achieving it, he was in fact just another privileged eighteen-year-old whose ego had been bruised by the real world so many of us are usually sheltered from. But Imran did eventually get there through a process of understanding his action and remodelling it. He wouldn't have gone through the danger of doing that if he didn't have a clear goal in sight; one that he believed was slightly out of reach but never out of sight. To others, maybe, but not to him. Then he set himself the goal of becoming the finest fast bowler in the world, which in the eyes of many he briefly ascended to, most dramatically during the 1982-83 series against India when he took 41 wickets and produced several spells where he seemed unplayable. Thereafter his goal was to be the best captain Pakistan has had.

This assessment of how good you are or indeed can be is critical. Imran talks about recognising your limitations and then working steadfastly towards expanding the range you can work in. It is an interesting thought. You first accept what you are capable of, which means you know how good you can be at that stage then work towards rejecting those limitations. It's like saying, 'I accept that my current skills will not allow me to be the financial analyst I want to be so I will work towards erasing those limitations and then become the financial analyst I want to be.' It is just as true though that a vast majority of people either over-estimate their ability or sell themselves short. Hence the importance of what Imran is saying: of knowing how good you are and accepting the situation before setting out to change it.

Two cricketers who were excellent at this were the Australian captain, Steve Waugh, and the champion Indian leg spinner, Anil Kumble. Neither of them was possessed of the kind of glittering talent that a Brian Lara or a Shane Warne had, but Steve and Anil constantly raised the bar on their performance themselves. Waugh in fact called his book *Out of My Comfort Zone* and Kumble memorably said, 'All his life Sachin Tendulkar had to live up to people's expectations, I had to change them!' Both set themselves very high personal performance goals and had no time for mediocrity — whether in their cricket or anyone else's. They proved that a combination of work ethic and challenging goals can lead you to achieve anything.

When we asked Sachin Tendulkar how difficult it was to live up to the expectations of a billion people, he said he judges his performance by his own standards and not by what people expect of him. So while the nation went into raptures over his double hundred in a one-dayer against South Africa in 2010 he didn't think it was that special for him personally. While he was happy that he could do it at the age of 36 against one of the top sides in the world, he felt that on a good day if someone had 50 overs to bat, 200 was achievable. For Sachin, a far more commendable record was his 35 Test centuries and 10,000 runs, something that was personally far more exciting and in his own words 'the ultimate challenge.'

Goals Can Overwhelm

One of the reasons people are loath to stretch themselves is the overwhelming fear of failure. In India for some reason, we look down upon failure, we regard it as irreversible, we push those who fail into a corner, treat them like outcasts. Wasim Akram, one of Pakistan's finest fast bowlers says, 'In our part of the world, if you don't win consistently, you get flak from the press or from your own people but in the west they just say bad luck, tomorrow is another day. We need to learn that.' And therefore the tendency to play safe most times. Ravi Shastri and Virender Sehwag are two other cricketers, who, despite their contrasting playing styles, showed the power of stretching. Shastri found that everytime the going got tough, he was being asked to open the batting but his approach was, 'If I can score when others are struggling, I show my class,' and so he took up opening the innings as a challenge and did extremely well in that position. So too with Sehwag who, after a brilliant century on debut when he batted at number six, was asked by Sourav Ganguly to open in England. At first he was hesitant but took up the challenge and became one of the most destructive players in cricketing history. On either occasion, if the player had worried about what happened if he failed, he would never have taken up the challenge. It is a great lesson for all of us. Who knows how many opportunities we might have missed out on simply because we looked at them in anticipation of failure.

However, when stretch goals are set too high they can strangle you because they may appear too large, too unattainable, too far away; quite like the feeling you may get looking up at Mount Everest when you haven't yet reached base camp one. A number of pharma MNCs reported that with the changing patent laws all eyes were on India, both as a large domestic market and as a manufacturing base. Sales targets that were set for the Indian teams left them overwhelmed and skeptical. But nobody really sets out to climb Everest or chase 350 runs in a one-day game because one runs the risk of achieving something substantial and is yet weighed down by all that is still left to do. The best players break down their large goals into smaller ones that seem attainable. In doing so they are never really chasing the large goal, only the smaller portion. And so there is hope and fulfillment on the way, the satisfaction of having achieved something and the inspiration to achieve the next goal.

Similarly the mountaineer attempting to scale Everest aims to reach base camp two and then base camp three. A team chasing 350 seeks to score 100 for the loss of no more than one wicket in the first 15 overs, then maybe 50 in the next ten. The challenge on Everest will begin on the last leg, while in the run chase for 350 it will only begin when no more than 80 or 100 runs are left and so on. The challenge for the Premiership in English football for example begins as a goal at the start of the season and is reflected in the kind of players picked, the quality of replacements etc. But the immediate goal is always to win the next game, or if the team is set back by injuries, not to drop too many points in the week. The hunt for the title, as an immediate goal, begins only in the last six weeks.

Therefore you need to break down the long term goals into a series of achievable short term goals. Having purely short term goals without a larger objective can cause teams to take short cuts, to 'just get it done with,' to do something that might end up hurting them, and in some cases even do something they might regret later. Breaking them down allows you to cater to the immediate without losing focus on where you are headed.

In 1976, India were set a target of 403 by the West Indies to win the third Test. Only one team in the history of the game had scored more than 400 to win a game and India weren't the best batting side in the world either. But they surprised everybody by scoring 406 for four and a few years later when he was asked what the strategy was, Sunil Gavaskar said the plan was to just keep batting session by session; at the start of a session to take care not to get out, then tell yourself you had done the difficult part and would be foolish to throw it away and towards the end to ensure you were around at the start of the next. The assault on 403 only began much, much later.

A good sales executive knows what we are talking about. When he is given the target for the following year, he can easily throw in the towel. But he knows that if he breaks it down into quarterly, monthly even weekly targets it doesn't seem very daunting. He can keep patting himself on the back for small goals achieved and stay positive about hitting the larger, more distant one. In effect, he ends up making the larger goal a by-product of executing precisely defined small goals very well. The larger goal happens!

Sometimes even the immediate goal can appear daunting and teams, or even individuals can run the risk of giving up before the effort begins. At such times it helps to present the goal in a manner that suggests it is achievable. It doesn't change the goal, instead it merely restates it in a manner that appears less daunting and provides the resolve to go after it. When for example Australia had made a world record 434 for four against South Africa in 2006, the immediate reaction would have been to sit in the dressing room with drooping heads and hope that the day would end quickly and South African players wouldn't look like fools. Instead, one of the senior players, Jacques Kallis, suggested that given the weather and the pitch conditions a score of about 450 was par and that Australia were probably 15 short. It broke the ice, cleared the air of despondency in the dressing room and set the mood for a historic chase and subsequent win. The comment didn't win South Africa the game, it merely created the atmosphere in which the run chase could be mounted.

Or again when India were set 360 to win the World Cup in 2003 against an outstanding Australian team that seemed to add a further 30 runs to the total by the way they caught, fielded and bowled. The dressing room in the break couldn't have been the happiest place to be in. Until Sachin asked a simple question of them: 'Can we score one boundary an over?' It's not easy but neither is it impossible. When he heard a few players say yes he asked what would the target then reduce to? A boundary an over means 50 balls produce 200 runs and the objective shrinks to 160 from 250 balls. Very achievable. Again it was the manner in which a seemingly impossible target was reframed that made it seem surmountable. It didn't change the target, or as it turned out, the result, but it put the team in the right frame of mind to tackle an overwhelming goal.

Mukul Deoras also believes that if one is up against a formidable competitor, the goal can be overwhelming. 'It's important to listen to what the person on the ground says and help him with the right resources,' he says.[2]

It's Not Always About Being Number One

Sometimes, small, precise performance-related goals can produce extraordinary results. This is especially true of people who are already on the path to success and need that little something to widen their basket of offerings. The off spinner might want to learn the *doosra* (the ball that goes away from the batsman), something that took Muralitharan's career into orbit; or the batsman might want to play the switch hit or the hook shot, a fielder might want to throw underarm with his left arm if he is right-handed. Often therefore your goals can be determined by where you have reached in your area of expertise; the beginner has larger goals, the expert has smaller, more clearly defined ones.

Normally when one thinks of winning, we visualise the number one position. This may not always be the case. Sunil Lulla, MD and CEO, Times Global Broadcasting Company Ltd, considers Marico a big winner since it stood up to a giant like Hindustan Unilever Limited and is considered a leader in innovation with brands like Parachute, Saffola and Kaya, each one a leader in its respective product category. 'You don't have to be number one, two or three any more. Even in advertising, there is place for niche, creative boutiques,' he says.[3]

Niall Booker, who was an outstanding country head at HSBC in India, and an extremely erudite leader, says, 'It is important to set stretching, but attainable goals. It doesn't have to be about being number one. For example, I would set a goal for the quality of our service, our return on equity, cost income ratio and implementation of our corporate and social policy objectives. These goals might not make me the number one bank in each of these categories but the contribution of these put me in the space I consider where I want to be. It is realistic for Tiger Woods to want to be the number one golfer in the world; it is not for me; but I can still aim to knock a stroke or two off my handicap.'[4]

Niall is absolutely right, for diverse teams at various achievement levels can set themselves different goals. The Australian cricket team, for example, could set themselves the target of becoming number one and in course of time staying at that spot. However that would be an unrealistic target for, say, Bangladesh. In their early years while they were struggling, their coach Dav Whatmore, set an interesting goal for them. Rather than setting the objective of winning a game, which could lead to frustration and disillusionment he told his batsmen that the goal was to bat out fifty overs against a strong attack. Doing that would be a battle won and would get the team to believe that the next goal was attainable.

Indeed, the definition of number one could be misleading. In the credit card industry, for example, profitability is perhaps a better goal to have than merely having the largest customer base. In telecom, companies might seek to have the highest revenue per subscriber rather than a larger but less profitable base. It is eventually about maximising the resources you can put behind an effort; which is why, Niall said (and was seconded by the former England captain, Nasser Hussain) that he quite admired New Zealand as a cricketing nation. They have a very small player base and given that, they frequently over-achieve, often punching above their weight.

Performance Goals Vs. Result Goals

That leads us to a very interesting debate about what kind of goals to set. Often we can get obsessed with the result for that is what guarantees our worth, indeed that is what we play for, or work for; that is what we hope will grant us our place in the sun, give us the best memories of our lives. And yet, the obsession with the result can become the biggest impediment towards achieving it. As we come closer or maybe encounter frustrating hurdles, we can get desperate; the calmness that is so important to our performance could desert us. We see this in sport very often, as we did with South Africa in Chapter Two, when teams on the brink of major success suddenly get tense and are in a hurry to get to the result, they panic and start doing things that are different from what brought them close to victory in the first place. Bowlers take eight wickets and suddenly look to bowl magic balls instead of continuing to bowl to their strengths and being patient. Teams play outstanding football for eighty minutes, lead by a goal and then suddenly decide they want to play out time. The defence gets overcrowded, there are panic clearances and inevitably a goal is scored against them.

There is therefore a substantial point of view that suggests that the easiest way to remove the anxiety associated with the result is to make it irrelevant, to ignore it, indeed not even to play for it but instead to merely let it happen. The objective of playing is to deliver peak performance, which is often in your control rather than to produce a result where you rarely control all the variables. As India's badminton champion Saina Nehwal puts it, 'I want to be 100 per cent at every tournament. I'm not concerned about rankings. If I win, my ranking will improve. My focus is on improving my game and fitness. If that happens, everything else follows.'[5] And so athletes should aim to deliver performance, the pursuit of which should lead to the result. For example, winning a gold medal at the Olympics can be a dream but you cannot control what the others are likely to do. The swimmer for example, rather than swim for gold swims for the timing, which is in his/her control and that is most likely to produce gold. A batsman rather than batting for a century says he will bat for three hours at the end of which he will most likely have got a hundred.

Setting performance goals therefore, not only takes away the anxiety of the result but allows you to come away aware of the fact that you gave your best. It's a philosophy shared by Viswanathan Anand, chess champion and world number one. 'I just turn up at tournaments and play my chess and see what happens. With tournaments like Linares I think you play to the best of your abilities and see how everyone else performs. This was my attitude in 1998, so it's nothing new I've come up with. I don't see the point of speculating too much. I just like to play and see how things develop.'[6]

For the truth is that there is no shame in losing after having performed the best you can, provided of course you are honest enough to know that you did indeed deliver the best you could. There is however much to feel small about if you haven't tried hard enough. And so the best athletes, as well as the best managers, pride themselves on performance and when they do that, tend to produce the results they wanted in the first place. For to lose is not a crime, to offer less than 100 per cent is.

Vivek Kudva, Managing Director, and CEEMEA Franklin Templeton India, believes that: 'Both performance goals and result goals are important. Without result goals, managers will not know what the end objective is. Without performance goals the end may become more important than the means and it may become more difficult to replicate success.'[7] The sporting parallel to that could well be that you think about the result goal before and after a match but focus on the performance goal during the game and in training.

'Actually coaches calculate what level you need to achieve to win gold or silver, but then break it down into small increments or whatever and give that as a performance goal to the athlete. In business, we need to convert the result goal into small activities and steps that the sales person needs to do on a daily and weekly basis. It's easier for them to understand.' elaborates Neeraj Garg.[8] Performance goals though are not for the lazy and the disinclined, for those who set themselves easily attainable performance standards, sit back and claim that they have delivered a 100 per cent. That won't take you too far. It is a completely different argument about whether everyone needs to go far in life but then real satisfaction only comes from being as good as we can be.

The pharma sector in India has undergone a sea change and with several new product categories emerging and constant mergers and acquisitions, calculation of market size and market shares has become a pointless exercise. 'The Indian market is growing rapidly, and the nature of competition changing due to new entrants and mergers and acquisitions activity. In this context, market share by sales value alone can be a poor measure of performance. One should look at other metrics such as size of business, share of a specific segment of the market, or even share of a customer group (hospitals, consultant physicians, etc). One has to use a metric that can be read consistently so as to provide a true reflection of performance,' says Neeraj Garg.[9] He says they would rather just set sales and growth targets for Nicholas Piramal.

In addition to the normal target-driven functions, there are others that play a supporting role but without whom the attainment of the goal, of peak performance would be almost impossible. HR managers, for example, in an increasingly stressful world, create a work environment that encourages performance. Trainers work on athletes to keep their bodies ready for peak performance. If we only assigned result goals how would we assess their contribution? Setting performance goals allows them to be assessed for the specific role they play.

Steve Waugh in his excellent book on the World Cup campaign of 1999, *No Regrets—A Captain's Diary*, writes that he told his team that it would be a 'no regrets tour'; that irrespective of the result, his team would leave England with their heads held high. 'Once in England, I introduced a new title – The No Regrets Tour – which reflected what I wanted from myself and all involved. Nothing left to luck, no "what ifs" or "if onlys", simply a concerted, full-on team effort that would maximise our chances of victory.' Not a single player, he said, would end the campaign believing they could have done more. The idea was that every player would deliver a 100 per cent every time he took the field or attended a training session or even, interestingly, a team meeting. So you didn't land up for a team meeting merely to listen and think about dinner while someone else was talking. If the 100 per cent therefore was good enough to win the World Cup that was excellent but if it wasn't good enough then so be it. The team would be proud of having done the best it could. It comes back to the truth that there is no shame in losing if you have done the best you can.

Setting up a Goal is as Important as Scoring a Goal

The thought inherent to Waugh's approach is that each player does the best he can for the overall good of the team. There is therefore an individual goal but it is subservient to the larger goal of the team. That is what all teams seek to achieve and very few actually do. In the heat of the battle can you pass or will you go for goal, and therefore the attendant glory, yourself? It is not an easy question to answer since sport, and corporate life glorifies individual performance within the overall team endeavour. We want to score centuries, the goal in the big cup final, the award at the annual sales review. And indeed we must have individual goals for that is what drives us. But the key is to ensure that such individual goals do not come in the way of the overall team goal. This topic has been dealt with in detail later in the book.

Team goals are often the result of several small activities performed diligently and successfully. Very few games are won by the lone warrior performing heroic deeds. That is for scripted movies and may it always be that way. Often critical roles are played by people you never see at the end. It could be a diligent finance executive who saw the need to restructure loans, a batsman who didn't score too many runs but blunted the opposition fast bowler, a left back who spent ninety minutes marking the opposition winger. These players could remain in the shadows, away from the stars in the arclights, but they know, as do the stars, that without them playing the quiet unfashionable roles, victory would have been impossible. Indeed, often a player may be required to fail in order that another succeeds. A pacemaker in a long distance race for example sets the pace early on to ensure that the star sets a good time but in doing so he has to bow out of the race before it ends. It is not a glorious sight but it is a role that must be played by one so that the other wins. One brand may have to bear the brunt of the competition so that another brand succeeds. That brand manager might have done a fantastic job even though his brand lost. The workhorse might have to bowl into the breeze so that the strike bowler can take wickets with the wind behind him.

These are seemingly unpopular roles and yet they must be played. In such a situation it is imperative that the leader makes it clear to everyone what his or her role is, what the successful completion of the role entails. If that role is clearly defined and is known to everyone on the team, and therefore there is glory in carrying it out, it becomes easier to play. Lance Armstrong, for example, could never have won the Tour de France without the strong riders on the US Postal Team riding just ahead of him, taking on the stiff, icy winds and leaving him fresh for his strong finish. If the mid-fielders don't keep floating the ball into the six yard box the strikers or forwards would find it very difficult to score.

In a situation where credit tends to go only to the finisher, the person who sets it up for him could well be tempted to ask for a reversal of roles – where one day he finishes and the regular finisher sets it up for him. In a manufacturing company, on-time production might well be the key to sales but if they interchange roles there would be chaos. Hence the importance lies not just in assigning roles but in the acknowledgement of their success. For every goal that is scored there is a goal that has been set up. If each of the eleven players wants to score the goal himself nobody will.

Production always sets it up for distribution who ensure that sales complete the cycle and bring home the revenue. The air force sets it up for the army to conquer territory. Bowlers bring down the target score that allows the batsmen to win the game. A great script writer produces the lines that draw applause for the actor. Somebody has to set up a goal for someone to score it and organisations that do not reward those that set up goals will find there are no more goals to score! Clear definition of roles and their communication therefore is the key to a great team performance.

- Goals are dreams with deadlines
- Goals can be out of reach but not out of sight
- The goals you set tell the world what kind of person you are

- What you achieve is a function of what you think you can

- As players become bigger, their goals become more precise

- Performance goals make you focus on the variables that can be controlled

- Individual goals must always be aligned with team goals

- Setting up a goal is as important as scoring a goal

- Clarity of the role and the goal is critical to winning

4

The Winning Triangle – Ability, Attitude and Passion

If you only ever give 90 per cent in training then you will only ever give 90 per cent when it matters.

—Michael Owen

'Business,' Jack Welch says, 'is a game and winning it is a total blast.' It is. There can be few things more uplifting than when mind and body come together in victory, in a melange of emotions that has no parallel. It could be the Olympics where you have waited four years for a moment that could have cruelly passed you by, it could be winning the World Cup, or the Oscar night where uncertainty gives way to the dramatic realisation that you have made it. It could be winning an account you have aspired to for years or it could even be the result of your first competitive examination. Just about anything. Winning seems to make everything worth it. Certainly, when you have played the game fairly.

And yet, winning is like a welcome drink going down your throat, like a beautiful embrace. It is brilliant while it lasts but it isn't forever. The high eventually melts away and the journey of life begins afresh. The truly remarkable among us visit these highs periodically; winning then becomes a journey, a graph where each point is crucial but is in reality merely part of a larger curve.

Winning is not a destination in itself but a series of destinations where fresh challenges are encountered and overcome along the way. Not everybody can do it, for winning can also be exhausting and that is why the true champions stand apart. These are people who not only conquer the opposition but also who conquer themselves, since winning brings with it its own set of challenges. That is why you remember Borg, Sampras and Federer, Tendulkar and Warne, Nicklaus and Woods, Pele and Maradona, Jordan and Ali. That is why you remember Infosys and Hero Honda, the Tatas, Hindustan Lever, Reliance and Bharat Forge and the many large corporations around the world who make winning a habit; not an event but a series of events.

Winning is fascinating to study because of the many shades it paints life in; the challenges of winning once and the many more complex challenges of winning again. That is why champions are extraordinary people, that is why corporations that win over decades are looked up to by their peers. While winning requires you to understand your environment, it requires you, more than anything else, to understand yourself.

Talent Alone is not Enough

The popular perception is that great players are blessed with incredible talent. They often are but that is not necessarily the only quality they possess. The world of sport is full of stories of brilliant talents that dazzled the world and faded away, shooting stars who attracted attention as much for their incandescence as for the brevity of their existence. The great players marry their extraordinary talent to something far more powerful, something more critical to their success. They are possessed of a wonderful attitude, a work ethic that causes them to chisel away at their craft, removing one rough edge after another till the polished diamond emerges. The romantic stories about sportsmen just landing up and demolishing the opposition, of mathematicians conjuring up beautiful proofs, of writers banging at their keyboards on a whim and producing a masterpiece are as mythical as Atlantis, the lost continent. They do more harm to young minds than anything else. As Dr Shailesh Ayyangar says, 'A talented individual without the right attitude can't be a long-term sustainable winner. A person with great attitude but with limited talent could still be a great champion member of the team. A combination of these two will make the person a real winner.'

Sachin Tendulkar once went to a Test match venue four days in advance to practice against a particular kind of ball that he expected to face in the game. India were due to play Australia in Chennai and in the warm up game in Mumbai he noticed that Shane Warne didn't go round the wicket to him even once. He's probably saving that for the Test match, he thought to himself and so hour upon hour he worked away at playing leg spinners bowling that angle, realising the need to be perfect. When the first leg break that he faced from round the wicket in the match was despatched over mid-wicket the world went 'wow' and raised a toast to his incredible talent. As we can see, it wasn't just that; it was good old-fashioned perseverance. Admittedly someone else with the same degree of preparation may not have been able to produce as stunning a result but it is just as true that without the effort, his ability might have been wasted. In fact Tendulkar's success recipe is a large tablespoon of talent but several large tablespoonfuls of attitude and of work ethic.

Talent opens no more than the first door, occasionally the second. Players armed with talent and nothing else struggle at the third door. By the time the fourth door appears they are no longer in the picture. The most striking, and sad, story in Indian cricket is that of Vinod Kambli who was abundantly blessed, had put in sincere hard work through very difficult times but struggled to adjust his game to the demands of international cricket after his extraordinary entry. He had the talent, but perhaps could not show the determination and discipline required to play at the highest level.

But people who are able to marry their work ethic to their talent rise above everybody else. It is the story of almost every successful person. Tiger Woods worked harder than anyone else on perfecting his swing, while Michael Jordan's training sessions are stuff of legend. And Lance Armstrong, who won seven Tour de France titles famously said, 'I don't win the Tour when I am cycling down the Champs Elysees with spectators cheering me on. I win it when I am riding in the mountains while others are catching an extra two hours of sleep.'[1]

But let us return to talent and the doors it can no longer open. When you are a 14-year-old your natural ability separates you from the others in your age group and allows you to be selected to the next level. Maybe you will walk through the under 17s as well. But by the time you reach the under 19s, almost everybody is good, and have emerged through a similar examination. Talent is a good friend to possess but not the discriminating factor. As Malcolm Gladwell so delightfully points out in his wonderful work *Outliers*, beyond a point it does not matter how good you are in absolute terms but merely whether you are good enough because by now other qualities become necessary. For a young batsman it probably now means analysing the bowler and being patient enough to tide over a good spell, whereas earlier his modus operandi would have been to demolish the bowler. It now probably is better to learn to leave balls alone till the bowler delivers where the batsman wants him to. Maybe he even acknowledges the skill of his opponent and plays chess with him rather than treating him as an opponent in the boxing ring to be knocked out as quickly as possible. There is this delicious story told about a 16-year-old Tendulkar who went to Pakistan with the Indian team and had to be told that at this level bowlers needed to be respected; it wasn't something he had ever worried about, because no bowler had really challenged him until then.

Young managers discover that their ability to find patterns in data, to produce outstanding funds flow statements, to devise complex algorithms are soon matched for importance by whether or not they can get along with people, by whether they can communicate to the rest of the world, by whether they can lead teams and display qualities of empathy, maybe ruthlessness. Lawyers find that their courtroom demeanour could count for as much as their legal knowledge, a surgeon's bedside manners could reassure a nervous patient. Ability brings people up to a certain position in the management hierarchy but now they discover they need to possess completely different or at least distantly related skills to go further up.

During one of our sessions for a top auto components company a gentleman got up to ask a perfectly valid question. 'When the company was starting out, they recruited us. We did well. Then, when it became bigger, they said we will recruit only from IIMs. Now they are saying we want to become a global company so we want people with foreign MBAs. What I want to ask is: if we were not good, the company would not have become big in the first place, so why should we not get the new bigger assignments?' In a simplistic world what he stated would be absolutely right. However, as you move up the leadership ladder you need a different perspective, wider skills and maybe the gentleman was excellent when the company was of a certain size, but wasn't too effective in a changed environment. And then, hopefully, he would have realised that it wasn't about an 'IIM' degree but about acquiring newer skills.

Resources Vs. Resourcefulness

Therefore it is not the talent alone, or the resources that players possess that is critical as much as knowing what to do with them that determines whether or not they become champions. There was a time in India when possession of resources was a differentiating factor. Few had access to credit and quality education wasn't available outside the big cities. It wasn't how good you were but what you had or where you were that determined your future. As a result, young men instead of setting up industries on their own worked for those that already had industries; cricketers who lived in small towns didn't have access to the best coaching methods and were in awe of the city boys who, armed with the opportunity that their birth and their address had given them filled up almost all the places in the Indian team. As late as 1983, India's World Cup winning team had players from five cities only; when we graduated from IIM-A in 1985 nobody ever spoke of starting out on their own. By the time India had won the World Twenty20 in 2007, players from nine towns were represented and fresh management graduates routinely dabbled in entrepreneurship. More and more students joining the IITs hail from smaller towns.

With high quality television, and good commentators taking cricket into the remotest parts of India, young players were exposed to the latest trends and the latest ideas. Armed with this, and the prosperity seeping into the next rung of towns — no longer fettered by self-doubt — young men, from smaller towns, more ambitious, more driven into doing what it takes, began flooding Indian cricket. Indeed they now had access to a resource that the city boys no longer had: time. And they had the space to play, they didn't have to make do with a little corridor between two large buildings. So whether it was getting into the Indian team, or into institutes of higher learning the tide had begun to turn.

We have now reached a stage in the country where resources are far more freely available and delightful statements that we thought we would never hear have done the rounds – that it was the idea, not the funds behind the idea that was critical because funds could be organised, the idea, not always. It has changed the way we do business but more critically, has changed the kind of people who do business. With resources being more easily accessible, and no longer being the differentiator they once were, it is how you use the resources that matters more; it is not who you are but what you can do that is important; indeed your resourcefulness is now the discriminant, to borrow a term from statistics.

This flattening of the world, this levelling of the playing field forces us to ask ourselves what kind of people or organisations we are. Are we high on ability but questionable on attitude? Or are we only moderately gifted (in relative terms, of course) but make the most of what we have? Are we therefore, slack organisations or stretch organisations? Do we rely on resources or on our resourcefulness? India's cricketers, or for that matter Indian industry turned the corner when they started becoming resourceful; when they became agile, worldly-wise and confident.

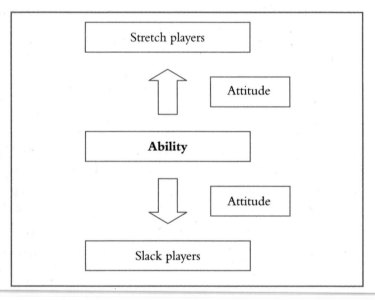

Winning in all Conditions

Maybe it is symbolic of their attitude, their adaptability, or indeed their resourcefulness, but good teams are capable of winning in all conditions. In cricket you will find a number of teams, who historically have been much better playing in home conditions, seem listless when travelling or playing in more challenging surroundings. India, for example won a mere five Tests out of 80 played overseas in the decade spanning the Eighties and Nineties while New

Zealand won only eight away Tests from 2000 till the end of the decade, seven of which were against Zimbabwe and Bangladesh. These were decent teams but the true measure of a champion side is whether it can win when things are arrayed against them: weather, playing conditions, crowd support etc. The two defining teams in recent times, West Indies in the Seventies and Eighties and Australia in the years either side of the millennium, won everywhere.

Good companies are like that too, always creating value and striving the most when market conditions are hostile. In a long bull run, everyone makes money, when insurance opened up, virtually everyone jumped on the bandwagon and made profits; when words like sub-prime were unknown you only had to insert the word 'software' in the name of your company to get the meter ticking. But as we know spring inevitably gives way to winter, resources start to thin and then your ability to be resourceful comes to the fore.

Australia showed the stuff they were made of during their outstanding World Cup campaign in 2003. They were faced with a couple of tricky matches at the start, against India and Pakistan, and were likely to miss two star players — Michael Bevan, who hadn't yet recovered from injury and Darren Lehmann who was suspended. On the morning of their first game came the news that the great Shane Warne had failed a drug test conducted earlier in Australia and was due to fly back home. Most teams would have carried that state of mind onto the ground, they might have pondered over what could have been instead of what really was. Instead Australia rallied together and produced one of their best performances ever.

And the confidence of having won in the most demanding circumstances carried them on the crest of a wave that brought them the World Cup. When the going got tough the champions had shown their worth. They had the bench strength but they were able to respond to a difficult situation very quickly.

The highly respected Cadbury company found itself in a similar situation in 2003. Just before the festive season of Diwali, when sales normally go up by 15 per cent, they were hit by the worms controversy. Some consumers complained that their favourite Dairy Milk bars were infested with worms. For a family brand like Cadbury, it could have been a disaster and for a while it was. But they addressed the problem directly, explained where the infestation might have come from, invested substantially in new tamper-proof packaging, began an exercise to rekindle trust with the consumer and in doing so actually emerged stronger from a potentially catastrophic situation. 'While we're talking about a few bars of the 30 million we sell every month — we believe that to be a responsible company, consumers need to have complete faith in products. So even if it calls for substantial investment and change, one must not let the consumers confidence erode,' the then managing director Bharat Puri said.[2] Cadbury had the resources but it was their agility, their ability to size up a situation and take immediate action that saved the day.

Australia's cricketers and Cadbury's managers showed that champions can, and must, scrap as well. It is not a quality that the hugely talented always possess; sometimes talent gets bored when confronted by a situation it doesn't really fancy. You will see that with complaining divas. But champions dig deep; when the first serve isn't really working, when the leg break isn't coming out of the hand the right way, when the wind picks up just as you are about to tee off and drags your first shot wide, they show the virtues of hanging in there. When the booming cover drive or the elegant flick through mid-wicket isn't really on, champions will scrape, nudging here and there for a run or just blocking for long periods. They are willing to play like royalty, even for a morsel of food. Everybody looks good when they are on top of their game but as Martina Navratilova once remarked, 'What matters,' she said, 'isn't how well you play when you're playing well. What matters is how well you play when you're playing badly.'[3] This is something we must all ask ourselves.

How good is the food when a chef is cooking badly? An article when the columnist is going through writer's block? While an average player looks brilliant when he is playing well but thoroughly abysmal when bad, a champion still holds his head above water.

Australia and Cadbury, like so many others, are examples of teams that achieved success consistently and success is the most powerful addiction that the world has ever known. The heady feeling that goes with victory is unmatched across countries or cultures and you really need to experience it once to get hooked. And yet we find that the first time round, difficult as it may seem, is actually easier than the sequel. Replicating success is the biggest challenge and those who have mastered the art of doing that are the true champions.

Passion – The Final Sieve

Finally, even among people who successfully marry their ability with the winning attitude, there are a few that make it to the very top. Sachin Tendulkar, Sergei Bubka, Michael Schumacher, Vishwanathan Anand, Maradona managed to reign supreme in a manner that they were synonymous with the sport they played. They were in love with what they did, had a great passion to perform. Tendulkar once said in an interview that his bats spoke to him! Their domination in their field meant that they set the rules and defined the category much in the same way that brands like Xerox did and Google does. Their passion, focus and obsession with their game and performance made them stand out as the best among the best.

There is a lesson there. Some of us are as gifted in our profession as Tendulkar and Anand are in theirs. If we can similarly marry our ability with work ethic and acquire the passion they had for their craft, we too could become the Tendulkars or Anands of our profession.

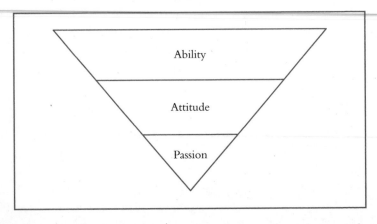

Contrary to popular perception ability is not a major distinguishing factor in success, especially as the level of competition increases. It is fairly evenly spread out across cultures and countries. It is a fairly large base of people. The first sieve therefore is attitude and people who can marry that to ability become more successful. Skills can be more easily taught, attitude can't. It is a more personal path. And at the very top is passion, an extraordinary drive, where success and joy come together.

5

The Burden of Winning

If you are succeeding all the time, you should ask yourself if you are taking enough risks. If you do not take enough risks, you may also be losing out on many opportunities.

—Azim Premji

That buzz in the dressing room, that electrifying feeling, team bonding at its highest, resources abundant and the overall positive mindset — the fruits of victory are many and varied indeed. It has a momentum that is powerful enough to carry the whole team or organisation with it.

That is the key because winning teams can wear the cloak of infallibility and have the confidence to take on any new challenge. There is an energy in the team that consumes even the bit player who has had no chance of starting; it envelopes the baggage man and the score keeper too. Magic Johnson once famously said, 'Everybody on a championship team doesn't get publicity, but everyone can say he's a champion.' In fact in cricket-crazy India, all is forgiven when India wins a series especially against Pakistan. Predictably it's the same in that country too! Then the coach is labelled a genius, the captain hailed as the greatest, there are celebrations all over the country, cricketers sign a fresh round of endorsements and cricket squabbles that normally make front page news are buried, at least for the moment.

Actually there is no better time than during a winning streak to strengthen pride in the team and build loyalty. Winning teams are magnets for those in search of excellence. What better team glue than victory to keep the herd from straying and looking for greener pastures. Smart leaders use the exuberance of success to spur their team on to achieving greater glory. Sandip Das, CEO of Maxis Communications Berhad, Malaysia says that the camaraderie in the team extends to even helping slow performers pick up. He thinks winning teams are, 'Apolitical and secure and back each other.'[1] Each of these is an interesting thought in itself. Losing teams by contrast can be racked by politics, have people looking over their shoulders and players who tend to put themselves first.

Looking Behind the Scoreboard

But if victory seems a perfect place to rest a while, you couldn't be more wrong. It's great to win but like all sweet things in life it comes with side-effects. Many sportspeople in fact refer to it as the burden of winning. Once you have won the world looks at you differently. The way you look at yourself changes as well. The next time you are in contest you are the defending champion with a record and reputation to defend. Pete Sampras first won the US Open in 1990, at the age of nineteen. When he lost the title in the following year, he said at a press conference, 'It kind of takes the monkey off my back a bit.' There was almost a sense of relief. He didn't have to wake up to the responsibility of being a champion, and with the expectation that accompanies it. When you are a first-time winner like Sampras was, you sometimes have the advantage of being the surprise package. Opponents don't know too much about you and hence can be caught unawares. Winners, however, are always under scrutiny, they are expected to win, their game gets analysed threadbare and the opponent comes armed with all the information he needs. If you are a challenger you make news when you win, if you are a winner it's news when you lose!

Federer losing at Wimbledon was an event as indeed it was when Schumacher crashed out or Woods missed an eight foot putt. It is not easy for winners to live with the knowledge that winning is merely par. Infosys or Reliance can report better results than most but will disappoint if they don't match the standards they have set. So too with the Oberoi and the Taj who must agonise over little things for fear that their absence is what will be noticed.

Sometimes though, winners can get caught up in celebrating the victory rather than analyzing it. After all post-mortems are only for the dead, aren't they? Jerry Rao, former Country head, Consumer Banking, Citibank India and founder and former

CEO of Mphasis in fact goes to the extent of saying that he is wary of people who have just come out of a successful project. He says they are 'all puffed up' and can go lax on rigour.[2] So the next time you want to hit the bar to celebrate, wait a bit and give yourself some time to think about why and how you won. If winning was analysed as much as failure, maybe teams would stumble onto things that they hadn't realized they were doing, maybe they could establish an activity pattern that they could repeat at a later date.

It is important therefore to know why you have won because if your own victory has surprised you, it only means that you didn't expect to win; that you thought it was a chance win, or maybe because your competitor faltered or that you just got lucky. Success has to be repeatable, that is what makes you a champion and that means knowing why you are winning.

Having said that, it's not merely winning that counts but also the manner in which the win was fashioned. Victories achieved under difficult and hostile circumstances carry more pride, are cherished more. Like away wins in cricket or away goals in football. Nasser Hussain was proud of winning on the subcontinent, while Rahul Dravid was overjoyed at winning a series in England. In spite of winning against Australia in India a few times, the Test win at Adelaide in 2003 and in Perth in 2008 was extra special. And the Australians look back at the 2004 series win in India with great pride. The Tour de France is so prestigious because it takes place under the most gruelling circumstances and is as much a test of character and team spirit as it is of cycling skills. While talent is always acknowledged as a quality essential to winners, words like grit, perseverance and determination are used just as often. Indeed in the foreword to Steve Waugh's autobiography *Out of My Comfort Zone*, Rahul Dravid wrote 'Waugh gave grit a good name!' Apart from the fact that it's a great line, it also provides valuable insight. While flair has always been considered glamourous, grit has never been fashionable, and certainly not in India.

Real champions like to play in adverse conditions from time to time just to prove themselves. Grand Slam winners have so much respect because they have succeeded in all conditions, have been able to adapt their game to the differing demands of grass and clay. Marathon runners participate in runs all over the world — in different climatic conditions, altitudes and terrain. This ability separates the champions from the challengers. In fact when the going is good, everyone does well but when the going is tough that's when you can separate the men from the boys — as with the cricketers who do wonderfully well on the subcontinent but fail on bouncy wickets with the reverse being just as true. This is as true in the stock market as it is in sport. Warren Buffet said, 'Only when the tide goes out do you discover who's been swimming naked.'[3] Of the hundreds of companies that sprung up during the internet boom, the solid IT companies survived and flourished despite the stock market crash (around the turn of the century) while several 'get rich quick' dotcoms bit the dust, their fancy ESOPs reduced to mere scraps of paper.

But let's return to the burden of winning. Once you have been labelled a winner you are expected to perform like a champion every single time. Often, not all successful people can handle the pressure that comes with these raised expectations. Since it is impossible to perform at your peak when you are under great pressure, it's possible for people to crumble and fall apart.

The Side-Effects of Winning

The media is known to be partial to winners. Their performance is dissected and discussed in full public view. With so much attention and adulation, champions need to be strong and grounded so as not to allow it to go to their heads. For you can run the risk of believing everything you read and hear about yourself, of getting puffed *up* as Jerry Rao said. You see that with footballers in England and, most definitely with young cricketers in India who are sometimes so much in love with what they want to hear that they only befriend those who tell them that.

Often, when the goal is daunting and the journey arduous, there is a sense of having achieved the goal, even if it's really only a milestone. You see that with students who work so hard to make it to the IITs and IIMs and experience burn outs once they get there. The real journey only begins once they reach there; sadly they mistake a milestone for a goal and they feel that their destination has already arrived. It is true of young Indian cricketers who sometimes experience such joy and relief at being selected that they are not ready for what follows. Even companies are known to become complacent once they become market leaders. It's easier for the number two and three to remain motivated since there is still an unfulfilled feeling and a higher sense of purpose. That is why managing success is always more difficult than achieving it, staying number one more difficult than becoming number one.

On a macro level, Australia began benchmarking themselves beyond their era in order to create challenges. Can we be spoken of in the same breath as Don Bradman's 1948 Invincibles? they asked themselves. The Invincibles were the first Australian Test side to have toured England and come back unbeaten. They won every single one of the 32 games that were played. Incidentally, it was also Don Bradman's last tour of England.

On a more micro level, Brett Lee says they trained as if they were number two to inject the urgency needed into a daily, routine affair. 'There were days when we knew we could train a bit and win. On those days we probably trained for two and a half hours or sometimes only for one hour but we went particularly flat out, pretending as if we were number two.'[4] A number of innovations like throwing with the wrong arm were introduced thereby making the otherwise uninteresting training sessions more challenging.

N.V. Thyagarajan, COO, Genpact, warns of another danger, 'potential arrogance'. Failure brings with it a certain humility and a desire to improve. We don't know if Bill Gates spoke from experience but he certainly spoke well when he said, 'Success is a lousy teacher, it seduces smart people into thinking they can't lose.' When Coca Cola re-entered India in

1993 they probably expected consumers to welcome it back with open arms. Instead, they faced competition from unlikely quarters. Pepsi might be Coke's only major rival the world over, but in India Thums Up, a homegrown brand from Parle was tough to dislodge. A few years later Coke bought out Thums Up hoping to fight Pepsi but when that strategy too didn't work, they unsuccessfully tried to kill the brand. Thums Up, India's largest selling cola brand, still belongs to Coke and was eventually given the full advertising and marketing support that it deserves.

Success becomes a blanket that covers up weaknesses. You don't see them growing until one fine day, the blanket is ripped off to reveal reality. In Hyderabad there is a popular saying, *oopar sherwani, andar pareshani.* In other words, the finery outside conceals the penury within.

Never Change a Winning Combination?

The success blanket is probably at the heart of the expression 'never change a winning combination.' It's tempting and so easy, so typical of human behavior that we've all probably done it at some point in our careers. Having won, no one really wants to rock the boat. Innovation at this stage seems risky (it always is but seems riskier when you believe you've cracked the magic formula) and experimentation seems unnecessary. Why fix something when it ain't broken? Unfortunately, it has sometimes started to break only we haven't noticed it!

In any winning team for example, there are a few under performers along with many over achievers. In fact all teams have their share of under and over performers. It's the ratio that varies across teams and decides how good they can be. Just because the team has won, it would be foolish to continue carrying deadwood. It's easier to cull when the team is down since it's not debated and anyway people expect that to happen. But it is just as imperative when the team is winning and the mood is celebratory. Australia did that well. They let a great sportsperson like Ian Healy go as soon as it became apparent that his time was up.

The underlying assumption in the concept of a winning combination is that there is a formula that worked well for you once and that it will continue to work again irrespective of how much time has elapsed between then and now and the circumstances that it worked under. But success is always in the context of time, space and scale, of when, where and at what level. You need to look at the context in which success was achieved. If that has changed, then the probability of the same formula working must necessarily change too. It might still work, but it is not necessary that it will.

Success is in the Context of Time, Space and Scale

Pyaasa was a haunting film but unlikely to appeal to a generation that doesn't think much of black-and-white photography, poetry and romantic losers. Bjorn Borg could never win Wimbledon with his old wooden Donnay racket in today's era where over-sized rackets generate such tremendous speed and power. Batsmen who were told to 'give the first hour to the bowlers' in a Test match would discover there are only 20 minutes left thereafter in a Twenty20 game. Alternately, sloggers who routinely clobber the ball over cow corner may not have managed too many against the four pronged West Indies pace bowling attack.

Eventually it is about giving the consumers what they want and those requirements may have changed. Twenty20 cricket is an excellent example of contemporary packaging for a traditional product to appeal to newer consumers. So too, the relaunch of Lifebuoy without its traditional odour. In both cases, managers could have stayed with what had worked in the past but realised that the reason they were successful may no longer be relevant. The passage of time is a huge factor to keep in mind while determining the relevance of a success formula.

The brochures that mutual fund managers send out have a disclaimer that says: past performance is no guarantee for future success. What worked at one time, as we have seen, may not work at a later date. What worked in one market need not work in another either. If McDonalds had to succeed n India, it could not do so with its beef or pork burgers, it had to invent the McAlooTikki burger to cater to vegetarians. Similarly, Marico had to modify its hair oil formulations and create creams and gels for the Middle East markets where the smell of coconut oil was not acceptable.

In days gone by England routinely played county seamers on India's dusty tracks and India brought four spinners with them in the first half of an English season when it could get really cold and spinners struggled even to grip the ball. A batsman who plunders bowling on slow, low Indian wickets may not always do well on bouncy or fast tracks. So success must be viewed in the context of *where* as much as *when*. For example Wimbledon and the French Open are played on different surfaces and with the exception of a few Grand Slam winners, only some have adapted to both equally well. Those who rigidly hold on to a winning formula are likely to discover that success does not last forever.

If there is a process that you used when production was at level x, it's unlikely that it would be just as effective at 2x, 3x etc. which is one of the challenges before small enterprises seeking to upscale. Apart from production processes, which is an obvious issue, there is also the question of manpower. As teams get larger, maintaining similar value systems becomes increasingly difficult as Deep Kalra, the pioneering founder of the popular travel portal makemytrip.com, learnt. 'It started getting difficult after we grew beyond 150-200 staff. While you hope that by hiring the right kind of senior managers and managers with the right passion and values and imbuing them with your sense of passion, the osmosis would work down the line. But it doesn't work that way and the training and development losses are quite high. Also every manager has his/her own style of working so things tend to get distorted as you grow bigger and are perforce not able to spend as much time with rank and file.'[6]

Young cricketers discover too that what worked at one level may not at another. While playing the Ranji Trophy they get used to receiving a bad ball every couple of overs which they can put away. At international level, they may have to wait an hour and so acquiring patience and the ability to pick the right ball to hit becomes critical. The style that worked at first class level may no longer produce long innings for them. So too with young bowlers who can sometimes expect to get away with a bad ball. At Test level the first one they bowl might be hammered away. Discipline with line and length becomes critical as they move up a level. And so success also needs to be measured at the level, or scale, at which it was achieved.

Not everything needs to be thrown out of the window though. It's a good idea to revisit what worked for you, evaluate what still works and then, discard the rest. That is why we believe that it is important to analyze success with the same rigour with which failure is assessed. If you don't know why you've won you will not know what change to make. As Sandy Gordon, Australian sports psychologist who has had many successful sessions with cricketers and teams says, 'Like all athletes, and coaches as well, we only tend to analyse failure. What I did (with the Australian team) was oblige people to analyse success a bit more — Why did you play well today? Why did you get a hundred? Why did you get a five-for? and getting people to reflect. Very often there is a pattern of behaviour, a pattern of thinking, a pattern of emotions, which many are unaware of.'[7]

The Perils of Winning

Some winners display a streak of arrogance and can start believing that since they were good in one sphere, or area of business, they would automatically succeed in another as well. Several successful sportspersons who tried their hand at films or politics found these professions to be a completely different ball game, not one that they could master very easily. Michael Jordan probably thought on the same lines when he temporarily gave up basketball for his ill-fated dalliance with baseball. But, as he discovered, the skills required in a new area of activity may be quite different from the ones you possess and could be of little consequence in the new venture. Organisations find that out when they diversify irrationally. Business houses make a foray into media ventures, for example, and meet with limited or no success. Companies with strengths in infrastructure may not succeed in the service sector. Those that have done well in B2B businesses needn't do as well in consumer-driven businesses. A strong presence in corporate and investment banking in India did not translate into a sustained retail business for Bank of America, and NDTV's successful news channel could not ensure a similar triunph for its forays in the lifestyle channel segment. Sportsmen, used to having things done for them, can find life a struggle after they have retired and need, in a manner of speaking, to sell themselves. They could still succeed but it is not a great assumption to make.

Success also comes with trappings — happy ones initially but ones that can make you lose your focus on winning. Net practice gives way to ribbon-cutting, photo-ops etc. Society has a way of heaping undeserved accolades on winners, making them more attractive than they really are. Winning a championship suddenly makes a player 'suave,' 'sexy,' 'stylish' etc. The perks and trappings of success make the champion forget what it was that made him a champion in the first place. It's difficult for people who experience a sudden upgrade in lifestyle and social status not to get carried away by it all and they sometimes lose it completely. Geet Sethi in his thought-provoking book *Success Vs. Joy* speaks of this. He says, 'Most sportsmen initially play for the sheer joy of playing. Somewhere along the line, some of them start playing to the gallery. That's when things go downhill. Once you start playing for what you think society wants from you, you get sucked into the sins of pride and arrogance.'

In fact, we often talk about the three related perils of winning: ego, over-confidence and complacence. Teams that win consistently can sometimes start thinking they only need to turn up to win, can look down at the opposition, not give them the respect an opponent deserves at all time. These are teams that are ripe for the beating and that is often why you see upsets in sports; why established production houses produce duds; why otherwise prudent fund managers pick mediocre stocks. In the face of ordinary competition, teams can mistakenly start believing in their superiority and can end up only offering 50 per cent. When that happens a time can come when that 50 per cent is all they can offer. Michael Holding once told us about Barry Richards and that he could see why Richards had been a great cricketer but also that he could see the effect of having played against a lot of ordinary opposition. That is why the key job of a manager or a captain of teams that win all the time is to maintain the hunger, ensure they do not slip into auto-mode, that they keep these three elements of self-destruction at bay.

Victory has a thousand fathers, it is said, and nothing can be truer. While there are many who want to claim credit, virtually nobody wants to accept responsibility for failure. The moment you hear of a success story, you will find relatives, friends, teachers etc. giving interviews saying they were the first to spot the potential, guide the young talent, play a key role in their progress so on and so forth. In fact successful people discover they have more relatives and friends than they thought they had. This happens with teams as well. People and departments claim that their contribution was most critical, the joy of a team win can get buried amidst the credit that various factions claim and so, in spite of the team winning, you sometimes meet disgruntled individuals who feel under-appreciated and under-rewarded. It is one of the many symptoms of what Pat Riley, legendary coach of the LA Lakers and author of *The Winner Within* refers to as the 'Disease of Me' which he says eventually leads to the 'Defeat of Us'. It is something good managers and captains must keep an eye out for.

Pat Riley's Seven Danger Signals

- Inexperience in dealing with sudden success
- Chronic feelings of underappreciation
- Paranoia over being cheated out of one's rightful share
- Resentment against the competence of partners
- Personal effort mustered solely to outshine a teammate

- A leadership vacuum resulting from the formation of cliques and rivalries
- Feelings of frustration even when the team performs successfully

Too Much Winning Could Be Dangerous

Some brands like Cadburys, Nokia and Colgate have been what we like to call 'chronic winners' at various times. These are brands that lead with a sizeable margin and haven't been challenged too often. Companies in such situations may not really need to stretch or struggle and they probably don't remember having been seriously threatened by a competitor. They are in the position of a Sachin Tendulkar, never having to go to bed wondering if he would make it to the team the next day. Let's say they can safely take success for granted even if they perform at only 80 per cent efficiency. That's when some chronic winners get into trouble. Competitors are not exactly breathing down your neck so it might be natural to take your eyes off them just for a while maybe. Abundant resources are available at your disposal so a bit of carelessness here and there can probably go unnoticed. The going is good so the team isn't alert in noticing new trends emerging. They don't need to because times haven't exactly been tough. So if a minor challenge crops up, the team isn't geared to handle it. After a while, the fear is that the 80 per cent efficiency level that the team has got used to operating at becomes all it's capable of doing. It turns out to be a case of satisfactory underperformance in the sense that the team is still winning. But the performance potential that it had is now diminished and they are ripe for a setback — and they probably haven't even realized it. The year 2010 alone saw a drop in market share of over 12 per cent for both Nokia and Hero Honda making both the brands look a bit vulnerable after a long, very successful run.

'Satisfactory underperformance', to borrow a term from management guru Sumantra Ghoshal, is a far more dangerous illness than might seem apparent. Apart from getting people to function or work well below their ability it can spread like a virus through an organisation. In a sports team, it could be the attitude to training and preparation before a game, for example. Just as young players emulate outstanding work ethic, so too can they start believing that it is permissible for talent to be sloppy. If senior players have late nights, you can be sure the youngsters will be tagging along soon. If the senior manager is loath to prove himself before his juniors it can lead to a cascading effect, which is why the old captaincy story from cricket continues to hold true: never ask your players to do something you wouldn't do yourself. Satisfactory underperformance is a serious illness with winning teams and like some infections, can stay below the surface until it is too late.

That is why Nitin Paranjpe thinks organisations need to have a healthy paranoia. He believes winning teams need to benchmark ruthlessly every time and the reason they sometimes don't is that they remain too internally focused, spend too much time and energy worrying about what is happening inside the company rather than what is happening outside it. His healthy paranoia, for example, is about widening gaps because 'if you don't, you don't acquire the tailwinds that will take you further. If, for example I reach a million outlets and competition reaches 500,000, if I then grow to 1.1 million I can be happy that I have grown 10 per cent but in the same time if the opposition starts reaching 800,000 my lead is effectively cut, my gap hasn't widened.' Healthy paranoia would seem to be a good antidote to satisfactory underperformance.

Winning teams can also get into comfort zones and sometimes stagnate in terms of growth rate. Along with creating the vision for the next level, leaders need to shake the team out of this plateau by creating what we call positive turbulence. It means making changes that question set ways, introduce external elements that break familiarity and openly address weaknesses or bad habits. It could mean resting a star player, raising the bar on fitness and fielding by picking young guns who make everyone else look slow, getting a different coach who introduces stringent work ethic norms, getting a consultant who takes an external, neutral view of things. It ensures that teams are ready for change should it hit them suddenly. In fact sometimes the environment forces change upon organisations but in case that does not happen, organisations need to be proactive in getting teams ready for change as and when it happens. Teams can get sluggish and complacent when not challenged and that's a surefire recipe for the beginning of the end. As Sunil Lulla says, 'Nobody can take pole position for granted.'

In fact, Nitin Paranjpe believes that in the FMCG sector (and remember, the 'F' in FMCG stands for fast, he says), like in Twenty20 cricket or even a game of table tennis you need to have your eye on the ball at all times. 'The price you pay for even a momentary lapse can be significant,' he warns. Ricky Ponting, Australia's cricketing legend but unsuccessful captain on the subcontinent wrote similarly after a lost Test match 'The little things, single sessions, opportunities not taken can quickly change a game in India. That partnership (for the ninth wicket between V.V.S. Laxman and Ishant Sharma at Mohali in 2010) not only cost us the game, it has cost us any chance of winning the series.'

So, as you can see, winning is brilliant, worth dreaming about, but only sustainable if you remember not to take your eyes off the ball.

Managing Success

- Success must be analysed with the same rigour as failure
- Success is in the context of time, space and scale
- Keep what still works and discard the rest
- Managing success is as difficult as achieving it
- Winning comes with side-effects: ego, over-confidence, complacence
- The Disease of Me can lead to The Defeat of Us
- Chronic winners need to guard against satisfactory underperformance
- Adversity separates champions from challengers

6

Learning while Losing

Some failure in life is inevitable. It is impossible to live without failing in something unless you live so cautiously that you might as well have never lived at all. In which case, you failed by default.

—J.K. Rowling

Bookstores are well stocked with success stories about Google, Yahoo, Coke or Nike. There are pages on what Jack Welch did right to create a winning team or how Richard Branson managed to build an empire or why Infosys became the success it is. This might lead you to believe that it is only the successful who can tell you anything worthwhile and that failures, big and small must only head towards the bin and don't even deserve another look. Of course you feel motivated when you learn from the stars but remember they don't always make the best teachers because, among other reasons, they seem to have the ability to execute even the trickiest of plans and, as mentioned elsewhere in this book, don't always seem to understand why others cannot!

Those wounded and vanquished in warfare not only have scars to display but with each scar comes a story and a lesson: of what not to do, of errors of judgement, of assumptions that were horribly wrong. Invaluable insights are gained on all that can go wrong and what setbacks can do to otherwise competent teams. It also tells you about how people behave under the pressure of a loss and why some teams recover while others find the burden of failure too heavy to bear.

Failure: An Invaluable Teacher

In India, people are very afraid of failing. In the US, people fail and move on. Here, you try to find ten reasons why you failed, everything except 'you'. In the US, failure is like a badge of honour. Oh, you have been to the war, you have been shot, you must have been a good soldier! India has to develop that culture.

—Dr Gururaj Deshpande, Co-Founder, Sycamore Networks[1]

In fact our attitude to failure, to a setback, tells us a great deal about ourselves, our organisations, our culture. In India for example, we tend to look at failure as a kind of death, a hauntingly sad tune that must play throughout our lives. The moment a player is dropped from the national team, the newspapers term him a 'Test discard', a terribly insensitive word. He is ignored at airports and stands alone in gatherings. It is almost as if someone from the flock has strayed and must be made to stand in a corner henceforth. This leads to a fear of failure which, as we know, is the fastest way to actually get there.

It needn't be like that though. A failure can be a friend for it can tell you where you are fallible, allow you to tighten your game, improve your career. The more mistakes you make, the more you learn about yourself and your ability and consequently, the better you can become. A friend of ours, outstanding at software and logic, argued therefore, that the person who only makes mistakes must be the most knowledgeable. Luckily mathematical conclusions are not always the most enlightening but it is indeed true that if you are willing to learn from your mistakes you become a better player, a better manager and are of greater value to your side.

Australian cricketer Michael Clarke was dropped in 2005, a year after an outstanding debut in international cricket. In most places it would have been viewed as a major setback but interestingly that very day Mark Waugh said, 'I said he'd be a captain in years to come and I still think he will be ... he's got a great cricket brain, It's certainly not the end of the world for Michael Clarke, he's just got to get back and enjoy himself.'

Darren Lehmann wrote in *The Daily Telegraph* that Clarke's sacking would make him a better player, just as it did for the Waugh brothers. 'It's not the worst thing that can happen. He'll come back a better player. All good players go through it. They've obviously made the call he needs to go away and make runs and he'll do that on his ear. He'll be back, no doubt about it.'

These were statements of faith no doubt but also pointers that you must experience the rough with the smooth. Much later Clarke agreed, 'As much as you hate getting dropped, it certainly gave me some time to re-assess.' As has been mentioned later in this chapter, initial failures can be like potholes on a road; in course of time you know where they are and can avoid them easily. By late 2006, Clarke had scored back to back centuries in an Ashes series, was made vice-captain of the team and thereafter appointed captain of the Twenty20 side.

It's probably predictable that most people and teams would like to take credit for success. But credit is rarely given to the role that the external environment plays in that success. All industry benchmarks come only from successes. Failure, on the other hand is the orphan that organisations and individuals are both to shy and scared to talk about. That is the reason why success stories are so well-documented while failure is strictly limited to post-mortems within the organisation. While the truth is that failure in fact gets analysed a lot more than success, it is often with the intention of putting the blame on persons, processes or even the environment or market conditions, rather than learning from it.

I've missed more than 9000 shots in my career. I've lost almost 300 games. Twenty-six times I've been trusted to take the game winning shot and missed. I've failed over and over and over again in my life. And that is why I succeed.

—Michael Jordan[2]

When are Teams at Risk?

It is entirely possible to lose because of external causes, reasons beyond your control. You might for example, lose the toss or there might be a storm or lots of dew in the second half of the game. In business terms, the recession, for example, had little to do with your own effort or capability. If you are in a business that is affected by government policy or regulations a sudden and unexpected change in policy could ruin your fortunes; a tax holiday on manufacturing might be removed or entry loads on mutual funds could be dropped. A change in market conditions could dramatically alter your cost calculations and negate your competitive edge. You could even be up against a competitor, who has an inherent cost, scale or sourcing advantage over you. In the mid-Eighties the Australians had to cope with losing players to rebel tours in addition to the retirement of stars. State teams in India lost the cream of their talent to the now defunct rebel Indian Cricket League. Technology might make your product obsolete faster than you thought it would. But these instances are relatively rare and more often than not, the performance of a team depends on its own talent, attitude and effort.

Around 1992-93, the Indian economy embraced liberalisation and there were sweeping changes in all areas of business. That era witnessed the demise of several top brands and leading business houses that could not cope with the changes and play with new rules. Some of them had got so used to running their businesses a certain way that when many sectors got privatized and more competition came in, they simply wound up and disappeared. Who had ever imagined that brands like HMT,

Premier Padmini, or EC TV would one day be history? Try this exercise. List the top companies in India in 1990 and then again in 2000, and see how much the two have in common. Of course many of the new entrants would be from new sectors like IT and Telecom, but many of the older brands would be fairly low down in the list for 2000 or may even have ceased to exist.

It happened with a lot of public sector brands who found that dealing with a consumer, or reaching out to him was something they had never needed to do. Interestingly it happened with some categories of imported products too as the quality of Indian brands improved. This arrival of the consumer, and the choice he now had was a defining era in Indian business. All along he only had a handful of brands to choose from and nowhere to go to if they didn't deliver on quality. Now he could switch brands easily and finally get rid of all the brands he didn't like whether it was buying an air ticket, a car or choosing a phone company of his choice. Companies that didn't adapt to this change declined rapidly. MTNL and Indian Airlines adapted reasonably but HMT, Premier Padmini, ITDC etcetera, didn't.

So why do some teams go into a slump? Each team has certain assets, be it products or people that deliver results, like fast bowlers for the West Indies in the Seventies and Eighties, or scooters for Bajaj Auto. They were the star performers. While they delivered, the team won. But at the same time, the team depended heavily on them and probably never imagined a life without them. The West Indies took the fast bowlers for granted and did little to ensure their steady supply. Once the generation of Holding, Marshall, Garner, Croft and the rest was gone, the West Indian team was a pale shadow of its former self. The likes of Ambrose, Walsh and Bishop kept the flag flying briefly but it was the dance of death rather than the sighting of dawn. The West Indies failed to build a supply chain when the going was good.

Overdependence on stars can also lull the rest of the team into underperformance. It's easy to believe that if you have a Tendulkar or a Jordan in your team it is their job to lead the team to victory as they do so often. But stars fade or retire, sometimes cruelly at one go as did Lillee, Marsh and Greg Chappell or more recently Warne, McGrath, Gilchrist and Hayden. Tendulkar, Dravid, Ganguly and Kumble were also of the same vintage. Teams must anticipate this inevitable development and prepare for succession well in time. Also, from time to time, it's a good idea to rest the stars and test the rest. This empowers the whole team and makes them believe that any one of them can take the team to victory, especially if the star fails on a big day.

In one of the finest innings played on Indian soil, Tendulkar was battling away with a bad back against a strong Pakistan team at Chennai in 1999. He was eventually out 17 short of the target and India lost by 12 runs. Many years later we asked Wasim Akram, then captain of the Pakistan team about his thoughts during such a tense match. 'I knew that if we got Tendulkar out we would win the game even if only three were needed to win. I knew India would lose the game in the dressing room itself the moment he was out.' An overwhelmingly big star can win you games but is not always good for the development of others if they are not empowered.

Phil Jackson, who has achieved as much success with the Los Angeles Lakers as he did with the Chicago Bulls in the mid-Nineties, has written (in his book *Sacred Hoops*) about the effect of having Michael Jordan in the team. Jordan assumed he had to win the game for his team but sadly, so did his teammates. In a crunch situation there was only one man the team could turn to, which of course, was great news for the opposition. Until everyone else on the team was empowered to win, Jordan scored more points than anyone else but the Bulls didn't win anything. Like Tendulkar and India, they had the best player in the world with them but it did little for the team.

Businesses too can become overly dependent on large clients or suppliers, or indeed, even single brands, leaving them in a vulnerable position. While displaying key clients or preferred suppliers, companies need to keep their dependence on them at the back of their minds. Advertising agencies have gone under when large accounts have moved away from them. ITC's successful diversification into hotels and FMCG products to reduce dependence on the cigarette business is a great case study.

Tata-AIG insurance relied on one institutional seller for more than 40 per cent of their sales. Then at the height of the recession in the west, that institutional seller aligned with someone else to sell their own insurance products. Faced with a 40 per cent drop in a hugely competitive market, Tata-AIG had to act quickly to build other distribution streams. They managed to do it but they had to struggle really hard for it. In doing so, they showed that sometimes the exit of a star can have a hugely positive effect on team spirit. Seemingly ordinary players can step up and display qualities that weren't expected of them; collectively they can discover tremendous strength and that is something that star dependant companies and teams should think about.

Bajaj Auto, one of the leading two-wheeler manufacturers from the Sixties right until the Eighties, assumed a steady supply of consumers wanting to buy their scooters. After all they once had a ten-year-long waiting list and owning a Bajaj Chetak or a Bajaj Super was almost a status symbol. When consumers moved from scooters to more fuel-efficient motorcycles suddenly the product offering was no longer relevant and it took Bajaj quite a while to regain its past glory, even partially. A team caught up in success sometimes fails to see the world changing. That is what happened with Indian hockey which was oblivious to the fact that the world was moving from natural grass to artificial turf which requires different skills from players. In 1975 India won the World Cup, by 1976 at the Montreal Olympics they were placed 7th, by 1986 they had finished last at the World Cup and in 2010 the hockey team failed to qualify for the Olympics altogether. India didn't change with the times, didn't get the right players and the right coaches and consequently lived in a time-warp.

It can happen with filmmakers too when they struggle to get out of a comfortable but increasingly irrelevant style. Ad film makers who make commercials for youth must always keep an eye on a changing world and must ensure that they have more contemporary people on their staff so that their style and use of talent remains relevant.

'Unlike in the US, we don't believe in the experimental model and are fatalistic about failure, instead of learning from it,' thinks Sunil Lulla.[3] Few companies and brands manage comebacks. He cites the examples of Star TV, Zee TV along with Amitabh Bachchan and Aamir Khan as media brands that managed to reinvent themselves.

That is why Neeraj Garg believes that a stable team has the highest percentage of underperformers. They reach a steady state and become exceedingly inward looking. Teams that do not have a fresh infusion of talent from time to time lose the outward orientation that is required in order to keep an eye on what is happening in the outside world. Even successful marketing teams can become large and unwieldy, and end up lumbering along unable to move swiftly enough to react to change.

P. Gopi Chand, winner of the All-England badminton tournament and now star coach to players like Saina Nehwal, was once asked why our women players, who look so promising in the initial rounds don't make it to the finals or semis said, 'Because they are well coached!' That might seem like a strange and unusual remark to make but he went on to explain that when players indulge in text-book play, there is no element of surprise in their game. They know exactly what they will do in a given situation but sadly, so does their opponent. Predictability can prove to be a weakness in marketing warfare as well.

Another interesting paradox is that a team full of winners often loses. In 2005, when it appeared that the mighty Australians were unstoppable, especially at home, an all-stars World XI was created to take them on. With no time to gel and with little in common to bond them together, they were no match for the well-oiled juggernaut, losing by huge margins amidst a media frenzy. Apart from not bonding, the other problem with having too many stars in the team is that each of them comes with an ego of matching size and, sometimes a personal agenda. A team of champions pulling in different directions can't become a champion team. A team pulling together is better than the sum of its parts. In fact the Australians often said they believed they were playing 12 versus 11, with their team spirit being the twelfth player.

Signs of Losing

So if a team is on its way downhill, are there signs that you can pick up? Are there symptoms that teams need to look out for? While every business will have some of its own to add to the list, there are some things they have in common. We have already discussed overdependence on stars. Another one is the reluctance of teams to accept collective responsibility for failure. Instead, they make an individual or some group or department the fall guys and pin the blame on them. Often, losses come during tough situations and one of the signs of a good and united team is that a number of people rise to the occasion, they are willing to put their reputations on the block and to take risks. In losing teams, members don't want to take decisions, they maintain the status quo even if it is doomed and would rather fail than be blamed. In fact in tough situations, losers like to duck. They feign injury or report sick so that they can avoid facing the challenge.

Many years ago India had an opening batsman who looked at the pitch on the morning of the game and always came back shaking his head and talking of how much bounce it had, or how lively it would be. He was setting the scene for a potential failure, almost laying the ground for it. Another batsman, who had done well in the build up to a Test match in Perth was told that, as a result, he would be playing the Test on what was then the fastest pitch in the world. On the morning of the game he hobbled up to the team bus and complained to the captain of a stiff back! The captain saw through it very quickly, realized that a reluctant player was not much good and told the vice captain to tell one of the substitutes that he was playing instead. Now normally, playing for your country should be a matter of great honour but the substitute, when told the good news, instead of being excited he responded with a 'Me? Why?' You see, he had seen the pitch too and realized that he didn't have much of a chance against top fast bowlers on a really quick pitch. Both players felt that it was better to sit out, to duck a game, rather than confront failure. It was never seen as a challenge, only as an opportunity to fail.

Jerry Rao says that a common sense of purpose keeps good teams focused on winning. Their attention is devoted to the market and to competition. Losing teams focus on internal structures, designations, perks, money etc. Togo's footballers refused to play their group matches at the 2006 World Cup over pay disputes and only relented after FIFA warned them of the consequences. At the 2003 Cricket World Cup in South Africa, a number of the Pakistani players were focused on individual records and there was no mention of a collective desire to the win the event. And the England cricket captain Nasser Hussain had to spend more time understanding the political situation in Harare than getting his team to play. All attention was focused on the politics around Zimbabwe and when England eventually agreed to play there, they just weren't competitive enough.

Sometimes teams that are doing pretty well can suddenly lose a couple of games and start doubting themselves. However a dip in performance does not mean that a team has lost its inherent ability to perform and become worthless. In fact the first casualty that hits teams when they do badly is their self-belief. They start doubting their ability and question their strategies thus far. Their confidence takes a beating, which leads to more defeats and that signals the beginning of the downward spiral. This is what happened with the Indian cricket team's performances overseas. After a few losses, the players stopped believing that they could win and like all self-fulfilling prophecies, it came true again and again.

Turning Things Around

To break this cycle, along with improving performance, it is critical to rebuild the confidence of the team. They need to realize that often being included in the team means that they are good and that they cannot suddenly become bad overnight; that the cliché 'form is temporary, class is permanent' is actually true. This is the job of the leader for he has the most important role to play in the turnaround.

In sport,the opposition understands this and that is why they often target the leader. They realize that if the leader has lost faith, or is struggling with his own form he will not be in the best position to demand performance from the others. In fact on *Masterstrokes*, Sourav Ganguly highlighted this situation. 'You need to separate the two roles, as a player and as a captain. If you allow them to merge, your captaincy will deteriorate.'

One way of overcoming this seeming lack of self-belief is for teams to celebrate even small wins to remind them that they can win and that it is the path to breaking the downward spiral. Niall Booker is a big supporter of celebrating even small wins when a team is down. He says the three most important reasons for this are that the team develops a winning habit, it builds confidence and wins attract talent since everyone loves to work with a winning team. During testing times, leaders often take risks. When they can pull off these risks, the team starts backing the leader for his courage. 'A good example for me was when I was bringing about change in our India business (HSBC). We got the opportunity to purchase around 15-20 per cent of what was then known as UTI Bank. Doing this transaction showed we could act quickly, move differently from our competitors and, importantly, be a catalyst for change. It sent a very positive message throughout the company, especially around the fact that the leader was courageous and could get things done,' remembers Booker.[4]

When Australia arrived in England for the 2005 Ashes, nobody gave the home team a chance, not even England supporters. Very early on in the tour the teams played a Twenty20 international and the English, in a departure from routine, came hard at the Aussies; they bowled fast and short and discovered that the Aussies could be vulnerable too. The confidence that a small win generated took them through the Ashes. At various times, players stood up and performed with gusto and for the first time in eighteen years, they beat Australia and famously went on to win the Ashes. It was a huge success but it began with a small win.

A team may be anxious to turn things around as fast as possible. But performance does not improve overnight, especially if the defects have been allowed to build up over a period of time. Everyone, including the leader must be patient. Sandip Das believes, 'When the times are good, stretch them. But when the times are bad, stick to the basics and be honest with yourself.'[5] Batsmen talk about playing in the 'V' with a straight bat, when they are struggling. Once the confidence returns they can get back to playing other shots. So even in tough times, there are things that you can do well. It is important not to let what you cannot do interfere with what you can.

In fact, teams, or individuals, that have acquired a negative or a defeatist mindset tend to focus on things they cannot do. They will spend a lot of time talking about a bowler they cannot pick, about a winger they cannot mark, about competition getting raw materials at much cheaper rates etc. Young fast bowlers might start moaning over the fact that they cannot bowl at 150 kmph, or a spinner can worry that he doesn't turn the ball enough, or a full back can keep thinking he isn't tall enough to counter the crosses from the right wing. If there is nothing you can do about it, there is no point worrying about it. Good teams and good players think about what they can do, about how they can get better at what they do, about things that are in their control. If, for example, an icecream company cannot get milk as cheap as Amul does, instead of giving up on the product, they could focus on new flavours, on a better retail experience, better packaging maybe. A bowler who cannot bowl at 150 kmph can, as an alternative, move the ball both ways at a fairly sharp 135 kmph. There is always something you can do. Good teams are patient, they keep chipping away, they get rid of the defects one by one. More often than not for them, the tide will turn.

Often, organisations condemn the efforts of the team when the desired results are not achieved. And sometimes this happens in the process of trying something new. Needless to say, every experiment, every innovation, comes with a risk even though it may appear only in the fine print. But if calculated risks are not taken, the team could stop growing. While failure is not fatal, over-analysis of failure kills risk-taking and that can eventually prove fatal. Jerry Rao says that there is a saying in banking circles, 'You don't get a promotion till you have made a few bad loans.'[6] India discovered that when they over-analysed the Sri Lankan mystery bowler Ajantha Mendis initially. Dhoni's advice to the team was to just go out and bat aggressively without worrying too much. That worked and the Indian team found out that Mendis wasn't as big a threat as they had made him out to be.

The key to turning things around is positivity – conviction that things will get better soon enough. In any team, there are always those who have faith in the team's ability and remain optimistic that the dark clouds will pass. At the same time, there are also cynics who are quite happy to run down their own team On *Masterstrokes*, Rahul Dravid talked about the team being like a pot, from which some take out and some put in. A team in which more people contribute is a more positive team. Sadly in a bad patch there are more demands to take out of the pot. The team needs to rally around the optimists (who are also generally the people who are doing better than the others) and the cynics need to be sidelined. It's true of individuals as well. Ricky Ponting speaks of the time when he was a little low on confidence after having failed to get runs in a few innings. He said he spent as much time as possible with Mark Waugh who was in good form and was very positive about everything.

India's badminton star Pullela Gopi Chand, on his march towards the All England title in 2001 ran into numerous cynics who told him that the Chinese hit too hard and jumped too high, that they could not be beaten and that even if he scored seven points against them instead of four, it would still qualify as a big achievement. Gopi didn't believe there was much difference between losing after scoring seven points or losing after scoring four. He said that he believed he could win and always surrounded himself with positive people who told him he could make it. He said he didn't have specific plans on how to beat the Chinese, just the faith that if he played his game well enough consistently he could win. As it turned out he beat a Chinese player in the semi-final and one in the final. It was a historic moment in Indian sport.

In the first year of the IPL, the Deccan Chargers were at the bottom of the table. An already disillusioned team got engulfed in rumours that the owners wanted to sell off their stake. The second season of IPL saw a new captain in Adam Gilchrist. He led by example and infused positivity into the team. In a single year he managed to create a turnaround and Deccan Chargers won the tournament in 2009. It is always a challenge to lead a motley, heterogenous team as in the IPL. The younger members of Rajasthan Royals who won the first season of the IPL credited their captain Shane Warne who always advised them to look ahead and forget about what happened before or to think of what might have been. Those who allow themselves to get caught in the burden of past failure find it difficult to pick themselves up again.

Actually, a small loss often does good to the team. It is a wake-up call to teams who tend to take winning for granted. It can also act as a gentle purgative — to remove flab, to reassess the team's assets and liabilities and to renew their commitment to the common goal. Chronic winners may not always be battle-ready and could be taken by surprise when sudden changes occur, thus small losses or challenges actually keep teams on their toes and prepare them for whatever the situation demands. We often talk about how good teams can emerge stronger after defeat because they now know where they are vulnerable. After the West Indies lost to India in the final of the 1983 World Cup, they returned to blank India out in the series that followed and then dominated world cricket like never before. Australia surprisingly lost the Ashes to England in 2005 in an era when they didn't know what defeat meant. In the next eighteen months, they had won the Champions Trophy, demolished England 5-0 at home and retained the World Cup without being challenged.

In fact leaders respect people who have managed turnarounds, who have clawed their way out of difficult situations. Adversity toughens up people, makes them dig deep into their resources and helps them understand their strengths and their limits. Sandy Gordon, an Australian sports psychologist, told us that in the Australian Armed Forces you often don't make it to an elite squadron unless you have failed and come back at some time for it shows resilience and strength. Saugata Gupta says, 'I would rate a person higher if he has either created something or turned something around. That shows character.'[7] During their great run in the first edition of the IPL, the Rajasthan Royals suddenly lost to a struggling Mumbai Indians team. That night their captain Shane Warne said he wasn't disappointed at all. He thought it was a good time to lose a game so that the team knew that if they dropped their standards they could lose. He thought it would be a great learning experience and could make the team stronger!

So, mistakes are invaluable in that they teach you lessons. They are like potholes on the road that you learn to avoid. Mistakes warn you about where you shouldn't be going and what not to do the next time round. Winning is not about not making mistakes but about how to learn from them and become wiser and stronger. It's not about not getting knocked down but about how fast you can get up and fight again.

Symptoms of Losing Teams

- Bureaucratic; delaying decisions
- Egos, internal competition, groupism
- Getting credit more important than getting the job done
- Lack of focus, energies spread thin
- Not enough back-up plans
- The same few people perform, no new people or ideas
- Too many or too few processes
- Crab mentality
- Blaming others or the environment for failure
- Weighed down by past failure

7

Change

It is not the strongest of the species that survive, nor the most intelligent, but the one most responsive to change.

—Charles Darwin

'If the rate of change on the outside exceeds the rate of change on the inside, the end is near,' wrote Jack Welch.[1] Great line! If your consumers are changing faster than the products you can deliver to them, you run the risk of becoming irrelevant. Cricket might have gone down that path if it had continued to offer only Test cricket to a generation that merely compares the speed of its gadgets!

Apart from the industrial revolution, the last three decades have probably witnessed more change than ever before. Dhirubhai Ambani's dream of making a phone call cheaper than a post card has come true. We can now get by without ever going to the bank or the ticket office or even carrying cash. We are in touch with hundreds of friends on Facebook but can't remember their contact numbers or birthdays. It's a changed life, for better or worse. The world has come closer and yet people have grown apart.

The technology revolution, with its cheap and easy connectivity has contributed to opening up global opportunities and access to unfamiliar consumer segments. This has changed the balance of power in favour of developing economies. The consumer revolution has been further strengthened by the retail revolution. This too has meant changing equations between manufacturers and retailers.

Slowly but steadily, a sports revolution too took roots in a country largely seen as a poor, third world nation with no imprint whatsoever on the international sports scene. While cricket is still the only team sport where we count at an international level, at an individual level we have world champions in shooting, boxing, chess, badminton, tennis and wrestling. We now have seeded golfers and athletes and even Indian-owned Formula One and English football teams!

And so, amidst all these changing dynamics, whether or not you can adapt has become a prime determinant of whether you can succeed or not. Over the last few years, some have managed to do it well, some struggled but finally settled down, but many others, like Indian hockey, resisted change and eventually lost. In this helter-skelter world technologies become obsolete quickly, businesses perish rapidly and people become redundant. It's scary and so people are having to adapt faster than ever before.

At 41, world chess campion Viswanathan Anand finds life challenging. The game is evolving and competition is coming from 20-year-old prodigies like Magnus Carlsen of Norway. 'You have to ride those changes, new approaches, new ways of playing the game. If you are enthusiastic and keen to learn, that's the main thing,' he says.[2]

Change Challenges Comfort Zones

Change is not an enemy, merely a challenge to a set way of doing things, a compulsion to get out of your comfort zone and go into unfamiliar territory. We live in a dynamic environment and so, whether it is a change from within or forced upon us from outside, we have to discard old ways of doing things and learn new ways if those are essential to survival. Eventually we discover that change is not the monster we feared it to be. Like bathing under a cold shower, using Twitter or learning to play the scoop over the wicket-keeper, we get used to it. Change must only be resisted where it invades a person's moral sphere, like in taking or offering a bribe. Old-timers, of course, think slogging everything over mid-wicket or playing the reverse sweep is immoral as well!

Humans, by nature, are creatures of habit. They get comfortable with things they use regularly, whether it is a bus route or a particular type of computer software; or indeed a fielding position, a batting number or a doubles partner! People get accustomed to their workplace and to the people they work with; to a locker room and a training ground. Familiarity breeds comfort. No wonder they get thrown off balance if there is a change in schedule or job description. Transfers are not always welcome and organisational restructuring is always viewed with suspicion. Tigers in domestic cricket sometimes end up looking like harmless puppies against international competition. Many established Test players initially found it difficult to embrace the Twenty20 format.

During one of our sessions with HSBC we were told of this outstanding employee who was promoted from the clerical cadre and was told he would now be a manager. His boss was delighted at being able to give him the good news and it came as a bit of a shock to him when he was told the clerk didn't want the promotion and he didn't want to change the comfortable life he had got used to. He didn't want to give up what he had for something he wasn't sure of. He was happy in his zone, like some people who are happy going on a cricket tour but not too keen to play the difficult Tests. Each of us must discover what we want in life. A comfort level and constant progress are enemies arrayed against each other. There is an apocryphal story of an Indian player who confided to his friends that if he hadn't been made to play Tests overseas he might have been able to lengthen his career.

Apart from the fact that change means a disruption of what you are used to, a certain sense of discontinuity, there is also a fear of the unfamiliar, like with our clerk from HSBC. As time goes by and you settle down in a routine, you become very secure of a certain way of doing things. Batsmen at number three like the additional five minutes they get to gather their thoughts, check out their kit and to relax. They don't like to get rushed into going out to open the batting within ten minutes of getting off the field. Conversely, openers like the idea of getting on with things rather than sitting around doing nothing for a while. They become edgy and use up all their energy in waiting. Each of them gets used to a certain way of doing things and doesn't like a disruption in routine. But, of course, the test lies in whether you can face it. If you can't, and a fine young kid turns up to take your place, you have nowhere to go.

Change May be Risky but Not Changing is Riskier

So will you be equally comfortable and successful with a new way? Fear of failure often prevents people from experimenting with anything new. There is also anxiety about adjusting to new people or processes. New technology (which has been the biggest change agent) can be initially very confusing and unnerving. If the older generation, for example (and many of us are either in, or entering that category!) who after great effort have familiarised themselves with some software or the other, are asked to upgrade to something fancier, there is bound to be resistance. Letting go of the past is more difficult than you think. And if the past has been fairly successful and rewarding, change becomes even more unwelcome.

As we have seen earlier in this book, if the past is glorious, we tend to keep living there, keep comparing the current spinners with the greats of the past for example, or continuing with a distribution system that is no longer effective. And if the past has been traumatic, we retain those wounds. A few years ago, when Dwayne Bravo, the fine West Indies cricketer, was told that the Australians, then undisputed world champions, were in a weeklong camp to prepare for the series, he looked bewildered. 'A camp? To play us?' he said. So accustomed had he become to his side losing. What a climbdown for the mighty Windies — and yet there it is!

It is inevitable therefore that the past impinges on the present. But in sport, as in most things in life, you *must* live in the present. The ball that has baffled you is gone and you are alive to play another. If you keep thinking of that ball, it will cloud your judgement in the way you play the next one. You learn from the moment gone by but you must act in the present.

Organisations that introduce change therefore, often encounter reactions like:

Have we been wrong all this while?

This is how we've always done it!

It's not fair!

The primary response to change, as we can see, is one of uncertainty. And of course a certain amount of apprehension is justified. After all, not all experiments succeed and not all innovations become hits.

And yet change is something that you cannot avoid or delay beyond a point. Change may be risky, but often, *not* changing could be riskier. Consumers change and so do their tastes. Singers who lip-sync might be okay and the need to acquire a classical base for music might be deemed irrelevant. If you watch old Hindi movies or even recordings of old cricket matches, you realise how slow and boring they now seem. We once tried to get our children to watch '*Jaane Bhi Do Yaaro*' and found they had lost interest within half-an-hour.

'Was everything as slow then?' they asked. We discovered why, when we went to see the latest edition of *Star Wars*. While to us it seemed like a special-effects showreel, the kids were engrossed!

Sometimes, new generations are unrecognisable from the previous ones and so are their tastes. If you keep your product offering unchanged over the years, it will get rejected, making way for more contemporary products. HUL learnt that when even a powerful brand like Lifebuoy which was a purely functional carbolic soap in the economy price range, morphed into a pleasant, smelling, fairly premium product that came even in a handwash variant.

The Tata Group under Ratan Tata became nimble and dynamic, ready to take on global competition. One has to change with the times, and what brought you so far may not necessarily be what will take you forward. Cricket's contemporary product, Twenty20, and the new improved Lifebuoy are good examples of an outside-in approach, looking at what the consumer needs, and changing in keeping with those trends.

The four fast bowlers theory brought the West Indies a lot of success but as the quality of the bowlers dipped they failed to find another path. As one of their legends, Michael Holding once said, 'There are no fast bowlers no more.... they merely run in a long way!' By 2010, fifteen years after a dramatic decline, they were bowling more overs with spin.

Success therefore needs to be put in context; in the context of time, space and scale — as even Manmohan Desai and Yashraj Films discovered with their lost-and-found or love in Switzerland themes! So you can only fully replicate success *ceteris paribus*. Accordingly, if the circumstances under which you had succeeded have changed, your winning formula will also have to be altered. Not all of it, maybe, but after careful consideration and analysis, teams learn to keep what works and discard the rest. The fine balance between continuity and change, like the balance between youth and experience or freshness and stability, needs to be achieved.

However, it is true that teams get tested during times of change, especially if skills, or attitudes, are deemed irrelevant. When Australia began their remarkable fightback from virtually the bottom of the table in 1985-86, they chose to rebuild keeping attitude first. It didn't matter if you were more skilled, but if your attitude wasn't good enough you had no place. It led to a fair churn, some good players were let go, but attitude became the foundation for the development of an outstanding side. Overnight, if you weren't possessed of attitude, or were unable to adapt, you were redundant. It could happen to any of us; the only thing we are good at might become irrelevant if we don't see the signals ahead.

Positive Turbulence Helps You Stay Ahead of Change

Sometimes, market situations, new technology or new competition can force organisations to change. We might, therefore, need to cope with change that has been thrust upon us from the outside. That is why organisations need to be proactive just to force themselves out of their inertia. When one is used to doing business a certain way and there aren't any challenges to keep you on your toes, it's easy to slack off and not be alert. No surprise then that the worst accidents take place on highways, not on crowded streets. Look at how the good batsmen get out against weak bowling in easy matches.

And the greater the mass, the higher the inertia. Large monopolies, especially highly regulated businesses or chronic winners are the perfect profile to exhibit such inertia. Such organisations, we believe, can do with a dose of positive turbulence from time to time. Positive turbulence is change that organisations impose on themselves, without any provocation from the outside, to sharpen their reflexes in their attempts to improve performance, like the introduction of Yuvraj Singh and Mohammed Kaif to the Indian cricket team forced the other players to run and dive in the field. They forced positive change on the team and improved the overall standard of fielding.

In sport, probably the most dramatic illustration of how a change in approach every few decades led to a higher and sustained level of performance, comes from the high jump. During the 1968 Olympics in Mexico City, most high-jumping champions used the style most popular in those days, called the 'straddle'. Dick Fosbury, not considered a medal contender then, introduced a new style, now popularly referred to as the 'Fosbury flop'. Like with most innovators, initially he encountered a large number of naysayers. Fosbury has been quoted as saying that the crowds would 'hoot and holler' when he performed his jumps. But Fosbury managed to set a new record in Mexico City, jumping 7 feet 4 ½ inches

— an inch higher than the next best competitor, Edward Caruthers who used the straddle style.

Between 1900 and 1960, the average annual increase in the world high jump record was one-sixth of an inch. Since 1960, it has been one-third of an inch.

Men's High Jump World Record

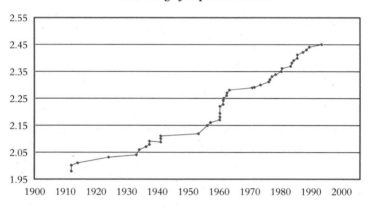

Change was most visible in Indian cricket with its embracing of the new Twenty20 format; initially with great reluctance but thereafter with great gusto. First off the block was the Indian Cricket League (ICL) and while it failed to make a major impact it spurred the BCCI to hasten the entry of the IPL and make it a grand success. The normally sluggish BCCI was quick to react to a threat and acted with alacrity. The timing couldn't have been better.

Test cricket was not finding too many takers among the younger generation who, unlike their fathers, were not a single-sport generation but had grown up on a steady dose of Formula One, EPL, NBA and even WWE. Even the limited-over format, they felt, was tedious, it took up the entire day. Twenty20 cricket was the perfect product for a generation which was low on patience and attention span, loved speed and result-oriented action. Twenty20 was launched amidst a lot of scepticism and even ridicule from the purists but in the end viewership figures showed what a winner it was and even the old guard had to acknowledge its success.

The IPL was an example of change at various levels: for the administration, who had to learn to live with profit-driven franchises, for the franchise-owners who discovered that they couldn't control every aspect of their business, and for the players who had to work with result- and analysis-oriented franchises. A conference call explaining a defeat was suddenly part of a captain's job as was a full explanation of his selection strategy. Indeed, Virender Sehwag offered a rather unusual, but for him compelling, reason to win a cricket match. 'Otherwise, you have to sit in a conference call. Better to win!' he said.

There was also a major change in the way Twenty20 cricket was played. Anil Kumble discovered that you don't bowl a four over spell, or indeed a one over spell, that you bowl one ball at a time; each ball generated a result, it rarely set up something for a later result as happened in Test or limited-over cricket. Batsmen like Rahul Dravid and Sachin Tendulkar who had grown up putting a great value on their wicket, who were never going to give it away to someone who didn't deserve it, now found that they needed to take risks they wouldn't earlier have taken. They had to live with the fact that getting out beyond a point was okay! Classicists like V.V.S. Laxman were forced to search for shots they had never needed to play!

It wasn't easy because change had hit at the core of their belief. Players who could play well for half-an-hour were valued above those who could fight out the opposition and conditions for a day. Even the mighty Australians struggled to cope, initially calling it a mere hit-and-a-giggle, unaware of the revolution that was coming their way. But everyone had to adapt because Twenty20 was providing a new, and significant, boost to cricket's product lifecycle.

Change is at the centre of growth and expansion. Businesses don't always grow in a linear fashion. While continuity is like the roots of a tree, giving it longevity, change is like branches that help the tree grow wider. How much can a company with a single product grow? Eventually, in order to grow it will have to introduce other products because the tide can go out very fast, as it did with such established products as the old-style film cameras (with the arrival of digital cameras and cell phones that took photographs) and compact discs. Cricket would have been faced with a similar situation had it not added the one-day international and the Twenty20 game to its product mix.

Even as you rise up the corporate ladder, job responsibilities change and new skill sets need to be added. Again, what brought you so far, like technical expertise, subject knowledge or capacity for hard work, may not be the same qualities that will make you a good leader. For that you will probably need vision, good instinct and great personnel-management qualities.

Former British Prime Minister Harold Wilson, who probably was witness to far less change than you and me said, 'He who rejects change is the architect of decay.'[3] Today, more than ever before, personal obsolescence is a real danger. When change happens, the effect is as immediate as the change of seasons. And it is not something that you can prevent or avoid. It is both inevitable and urgent. The more you delay or resist it, the more time you have lost. It is also a myth that the leader in the team normally leads change. Two of the greatest changes to the limited overs game came from those playing minor roles.

Before the World Cup of 1996, Sri Lanka were not among the powers of the game but their opening batsmen redefined the way limited overs cricket would be played. Romesh Kaluwitharana and Sanath Jayasuriya batted aggressively from the word go, making full use of the fielding restrictions in the first 15 overs and making them look like slog overs. In subsequent years, other teams had no choice but to follow the trend that the Sri Lankans had set in 1996. A few years later a cricketer called Douglas Marillier from Zimbabwe started hopping across to off stump to scoop full length balls over short fine leg. Tilakaratne Dilshaan modified the 'Marillier' or 'paddle scoop' as it came to be known, hitting the ball straight over the wicket-keeper's head and creating his own 'Dilscoop' — another example of change emerging from the lower echelons.

In fact, today, smaller companies are more agile and nimble and in a far better position to introduce innovation. And if the leader is caught napping, this could mean trouble. Imagine a terrific packaging innovation introduced by a smaller player, along the lines of what Cavin Kare did with sachets in the shampoo market. A market leader who is following the change, not leading it, can be stuck with a whole stock of old packaging before he can copy the new one. 'However, if a giant is the first to introduce the change, just imagine the momentum,' points out Nitin Paranjpe.[4]

Teams that practice positive turbulence can stay ahead of the change. Like hackers who test a company's security systems or Google-staffers who are given time to develop their own projects, maybe the day is not far when companies hire people to see if disruptive change can be beneficial.

Change Needs Ambassadors

So if change is inevitable yet risky, urgently required and yet uncomfortable, how does a leader steer his team through a turbulent phase? How does he ensure that the blueprint of restructuring or reorganisation gets executed well at all levels? Firstly, the leader must have complete conviction about the plan. If he or she hems and haws over it, there is no chance that the plan will succeed. The next step is to get a buy-in from the entire team. And for that the leader must almost be an evangelist; for there will be resistance from key stakeholders.

We did a session for a large auto company where the objective was to set ambitious growth targets and the company needed the dealers to change with them to achieve the targets. It meant changing the way showrooms looked and hiring smarter people to service clients, among other things. They ran into a bit of a roadblock with the dealers who said that theirs was a time-tested method since they knew each of their customers on a personal level. They were loath to let go of this old-world approach which had worked very well up to a certain point but wasn't practical if the new ambitious sales figures had to be achieved. It required great persuasive skills from the leader to get the message across!

The key to this acceptance of change is in the change initiator addressing the all-important question: What's in it for me? There has to be an exciting and inviting game plan that has to be communicated to the team in the most inspiring fashion. Even then, there will be skeptics who will run down all ideas. There will be some doubters who will need some more convincing. Sometimes, the old guard can feel insecure, as we discovered with an organisation where an expatriate CEO had arrived to drive change. In one of our sessions, we gave them a slightly modified version of the Greg Chappell-Sourav Ganguly situation where an external change agent was trying to bring about drastic change. The younger, more ambitious employees bought into the need for change very easily, while the senior managers, much like a couple of India's senior cricketers, resisted it out of insecurity. It was a learning experience for the CEO to see such a clear divide when change was in the air, and helped him address the situation better.

In fact, Neeraj Garg says that organisations must have younger players who will keep the older players aware of changing trends, like Yuvraj and Kaif did with their sliding and diving in the field. And then there will be the optimists, the enthusiasts who have to be used as change ambassadors. Change multiplies geometrically if there are enough people with a 'can do' attitude, which is why the role of the change ambassadors becomes important. This is especially true of large organisations where a changed mission statement might emerge out of a boardroom in Mumbai but will have to be implemented in places like Villupuram and Sonepat.

Often, companies bring in outsiders as change agents since outsiders come with no baggage about the new organisation and bring in a fresh perspective. What they also bring in often, is their own groupies from the old company. There is a fear that an Us vs. Them situation can arise, especially during this stage that anyway is fraught with anxiety and uncertainty. You see that in football all the time; for example, when an Italian manager takes over an English team. He brings with him an assistant manager, a trainer, a physiotherapist and the like, and a situation could well develop where the players might say 'Hang on, who is the team? Is it us English or them Italians?'

A time of change comes with several challenges for the team and these are only some of them. A team that makes the changeover successfully and optimistically is likely to make its bonds stronger in the process.

Indian Hockey

In cricket-crazy India, most people are not even aware that it is hockey that is designated as our national sport. In 1928, India won its first Olympic gold medal. From 1928 to 1956, the Indian men's team remained unbeaten in the Olympics, garnering six gold medals in a row. That was also the golden era of Indian hockey when the magic of the legendary Dhyan Chand took the game to dizzying heights. The Indian team has won a total of eight gold, one silver and two bronze medals in the Olympics. In March 2008, India lost 2-0 to Britain at Santiago, Chile, failing to qualify for the Beijing Olympics, a humiliating 'first' for a country with such a glorious tradition in the game.

In the World Cup held in March 2010, India finished eighth from amongst 12 countries. Immediately, two senior players Prabhjot Singh and Deepak Thakur were dropped from the Azlan Shah Cup, supposedly on grounds of a poor showing in the World Cup but amidst speculation that they had been left out because of their role in the players' revolt over wages before the World Cup. The last few years has seen Indian hockey in the news for all the wrong reasons — in-fighting in the Indian Hockey Federation, controversies regarding the hiring and sacking of coaches, unrest among players on issues relating to facilities, wages etc. The team appears to be in a poor mental state and 'losing respectably' to teams like Australia seems an acceptable option.

The story of Indian hockey in the last three decades is one of refusal to embrace change, leaving too much till too late and not having a process in place even when change was recognised as something that was inevitable.

Change doesn't let you wait and watch: The game that Indians were champions at 50 years ago is not the same as the one that is played today. In those days, hockey was played on grass and the Indian style of wristy shots and pretty moves was perfect for the surface. Europe, home to Astroturf surfaces, was the earliest to move to the artificial surface, about 40 years ago. Today, Holland has 900 such grounds, Australia has about 300, with Melbourne alone having about 30. In comparison, India now has about 40 astroturfs, mainly in the north, from where the largest number of players come, with Mumbai having only one. Viren Rasquinha, former India hockey captain, who now runs Olympic Gold Quest, a company formed by former champions like Prakash Padukone and Geet Sethi with the objective of spotting and grooming potential Olympic medal-winners, says the techniques required on the two surfaces are completely different and if players are not used to the surface right from a junior level, making the transition is very difficult. Viren's club in Germany alone had four astroturfs. Today, the game is all about power, agility and fitness.

The current lot of Indian players are aware of the changes required but don't have the right trainers and support staff to guide them. Training has become very specialised and international sides like Germany and Australia, the two finalists at the World Cup held in India (in 2010) earlier this year, have world-class technology and experts to analyse the data available. Since fitness is so important, backup support in terms of physiotherapists and nutritionists is integral to the team. Match fitness is different from general fitness and Indian trainers lack training in these aspects.

Harping on our glorious past, apart from imposing an emotional burden on them, means precious little to players who were not even born then.

Change cannot be half-hearted, it needs a process: It's not as if no attempts have been made to modernise the game in our country. But attempts that aim only at the top of the pyramid cannot have effects that are either substantial or lasting. Errors that are allowed in domestic hockey, which is of a poor standard, appear greatly magnified at the international level. The emphasis on fitness and proper training techniques has to happen from the initial stages, which means that state-of-the-art infrastructure and competent trainers need to be available even in the smaller centres.

Training very hard but not really smart does not yield the desired result and can actually be counter-productive since it leads to a demoralised side.

The focus must be on winning and winning alone: For decades now, the hockey establishment has been run by politicians, former bureaucrats and retired players, none of whom could really contribute towards better performance in the game. Mismanagement, in-fighting and lack of a professional approach have turned potential sponsors and broadcasters away from the game. Moreover, all these are honorary posts which means that only players and coaches get sacked for poor performance, not officials. 'Honorary jobs only give honorary results,' says Viren Rasquinha. So in spite of having loads of raw talent in the country, hockey is mired in constant controversy. Instead of the focus being on winning, it is on the power struggles of officials, the sudden hiring and firing of coaches (which again means no accountability), player unrest and post mortems in the media after every poor showing.

8

Team Building

While the current thinking in business schools holds that all someone with an idea needs to succeed are focus, clarity and a good business plan, I have found that bringing together a great team that's united by strong motivation, determination and bravery is much more important.

—Richard Branson

One of the favourite past-times of sports-lovers is picking their dream teams. We've all done it and experienced the great power of holding someone's destiny in our hands! But picking a dream team is really picking the best man for the position at that time, ideally an all-time great. The best thing about this exercise, apart from the fact that the 'team' is never going to take the field, is that nobody needs to give thought to issues like how a Garry Sobers could communicate with an Umar Gul for example, or whether Don Bradman would get along with Muttiah Muralitharan. Could Pele and Maradona have co-existed in the same team? How would Jayawardene have handled Shoaib Akhtar? All you know is that you have a team of your choice, or more precisely a collection of players, that you believe will be a winner.

In corporate life though, there is a major difference. Unless you are a start-up, most leaders inherit teams and these teams may not always be ideal. Most leaders wish their teams were like Manchester United or Barcelona playing together and generating quality performances day in and day out. Managers too aspire to work for top notch companies — say an Infosys or a Wipro — because these organisations are seen as 'winning teams'. But while it's easy to spot a winning team or an employer of choice, building a champion side is unfortunately not as easy as picking your Dream Team.

The challenge is in knowing what makes these dream teams work, how we can make our team the Manchester United of retailing, for example, or how to transform our bank into the Chelsea of finance — for these are merely symbols of well-oiled, successful units.

The Building Blocks — Talent, Team Climate and Collective Pride

Very often, execution is the defining element and therefore the stumbling-block. It is one thing to know what to do, quite another to actually put that into practice. To be able to do that, you need good teams with good team-players, because quality execution often requires one set of people to help another set to deliver. The team must possess that work ethic and the players must be happy enough to follow it. So whether you are making a film, playing a competitive sport or running a company, the same three things go into making a good team; great talent, a healthy team climate that is conducive to performance, and collective pride. Contrary to what we have been made to believe in our growing-up years, talent counts for the least. It can stagnate and rot when not nurtured properly but bloom and mature under the right conditions. Pride in the team ensures that success is not one-time and the flock stays together happily to see many more wins.

Success is the magnet that attracts talent and resources. Performers want to work for companies that are on the list of best employers, and companies want to be employers of choice. Venture capitalists are interested in fledgling companies that hold promise, clients want to associate themselves with big names, and suppliers in turn like to flaunt their top clients. It might seem like a chicken-and-egg situation but everyone wants winners or, it seems, at least to search for them!

The aura around winners is unmistakable, whether it's the swagger of a Viv Richards or Vijay Mallya, the cool confidence of a Roger Federer or Steve Jobs, the cockiness of Usain Bolt or Richard Branson or the understated charm of Ratan Tata or Vishwanathan Anand. But winners need to be in the right company as well. Thierry Henry didn't perform for France as well as he did for Arsenal;

Andrei Shevchenko was brilliant at AC Milan and disastrous at Chelsea. Directors make good films only with certain producers and interestingly, successful CEOs sometimes fail to recreate the magic when they move jobs.

It is interesting to try and see why that happens. The essence of good teams, as we have seen, lies in the sense of belonging, in the ability to play for each other. And yet, people who possess all this find the urge to move jobs. Essentially people move because they are offered better terms somewhere else; they perceive a greater challenge, see greater power for themselves maybe, or they seek to fulfil an aspiration. There is nothing wrong with any of these and indeed, people have made some very good moves for these reasons but they need to be very sure that they will fit into a new set-up, into a fresh team ethic, wherever they go.

Coaches and corporate leaders are very often quoted as saying that they place attitude over talent. Talent is always easier to find since all our education is geared towards teaching us skills. But talent without the right attitude is like a stallion running amuck. Even though it is over-rated, a team will struggle without talent. But a player's attitude or a collection of player attitudes defines team spirit and determines where the team ends up. People who build good teams tend to use talent, or ability, as the first cut-off but thereafter strive strenuously to mould that ability into a strong team ethic. Alex Ferguson does that at Manchester United and captains and coaches have made that a benchmark for Australian cricket.

Surrendering the Me for the We

Attitude needs to be cultivated long-term and good teams are quick to encourage and reward good attitude while nipping errant behaviour in the bud. Pat Riley says that good teams become great when players trust each other enough to surrender the 'me' for the 'we'. It's an engaging thought. On the surface it doesn't seem like a long distance to cover but it can be frightfully long for some teams. Often, teams that seek to make a place for themselves in the sun, start up entrepreneurial ventures; teams inching their way up the leagues display tremendous zeal and are united by the all-for-one-and-one-for-all approach. The biggest danger to the 'we' ironically comes with winning. Think about it. The pursuit of success brings a team together but achieving it can sometimes be a poison pill and test a leader.

Success, as we know, often breeds many failures. 'I took the two wickets that triggered the collapse, the bowler might say. The defence might claim that their steadfastness prevented a goal being scored while the striker might point to the fact that eventually someone had to put the ball into the net. The hallmark of a good leader lies, therefore, not just in building a team but holding it together when the call for individual glory is sounded by some. That is why good leaders often point to trust as the most important ingredient in building a good team.

One of the biggest issues that Human Resources managers in India are dealing with is that Indians don't make very good team-players. Mathew Hayden raised a storm when he said that Indian cricketers are selfish and play for personal milestones. 'But countries like India suffer from that. We back ourselves against those countries because they'll get two or three players in the 70s and beyond, and they'll be eyeing off that personal landmark and it'll cost their side 40 or 50 runs as a result... In one-day cricket, the so-called landmarks like 50s and 100s are not achieved at the same rate as in Tests... it's partnerships that can really hurt a side and set up a side.'

But Hayden wasn't wrong. Because there was a phase in Indian cricket when the batsmen scored more centuries than anyone else but the team itself didn't have a record to match. By contrast, of the initial quartet of West Indies fast bowlers, Andy Roberts, Michael Holding, Joel Garner and Colin Croft, not one of them took 300 Test wickets — but collectively they were a lethal force.

A popular explanation for this phenomenon is that our large population forces us to develop selfish instincts at every step. You cannot get into a bus or a train if you make way for someone else. And with the amount of domestic cricket in India, selectors often look at individual scores rather than the situation they were played in. A gritty 32 when the team is in trouble may be more valuable than an 80 on a flat pitch against poor opposition, but inevitably the player who gets the 80 will catch the selector's eye if he hasn't been at the ground. In such a climate, a player who has become conditioned to put 'self' first is suddenly expected to subjugate his needs to those of the team when he plays at the national level. It cannot happen and therein maybe lies an explanation for Hayden's observation.

One hypothesis is that in over-populated, and therefore insecure countries, the self will always dominate. Feelings of comradeship, of surrendering the self to the wider cause, can only arise in either a highly spiritual phase or where the performer has ascended to a level of personal calm about his achievements. When you are in a mob, and all of us are in a mob sometimes, self-preservation will always prevail. But when a team is performing, and therefore settled, and where individuals are secure, they can rise above the self and play for the cause. Indeed, playing for the cause then becomes a greater virtue.

Indians have to constantly compete for limited seats in both education and jobs. Marten Pieters, MD and CEO of Vodafone Essar, likes to think of Indians as individualistic rather than selfish. 'People are individualistic in all cultures. But in India you learn very young that you can only succeed more or less at the cost of someone else. Here you are happy to scream from the towers, 'I am the best of the class'. If you did that in Holland, people would hate you. It is more appreciated to be in line with the team than excel.'[1]

One of the clues to how good a team-player you are lies in how much you are willing to do for no reward, how hard you are willing to run as a non-striker or how much you are willing to push yourself to cut off a boundary or save a run. These are things that contribute to the performance of the team or your teammate, but not to your personal figures. We asked Sachin how, as a captain and senior player, he evaluated players. It came as no surprise that the ultimate team-player said without any hesitation that he rates players by their commitment, rather than their performance. He says that effort is the only thing entirely in your control and that he has no respect for those unwilling to put that in.

Jerry Rao thinks that the punishment for flouting team rules in our part of the world is very low. Witness politicians being readmitted after being expelled, players seemingly left out on disciplinary grounds picked for big games. Clearcut communication of team rules and a low tolerance for deviation from these rules are critical to good team culture.

In their best years as a team, Pakistan were led by Imran Khan, who demanded a very high standard of team ethic. The story goes that in one of their always highly charged games against India at Sharjah, a batsmen was sent out with clear instructions to go for it in the last two overs. But not having done too well in the earlier games the player was probably a bit insecure and opted to return not out rather than go with the riskier alternative of attacking and, maybe, getting out. As the players returned to the pavilion for lunch, Imran came down the steps towards the boundary rope and told the batsman loudly enough for everyone to hear, 'You will never play for Pakistan again'. The message was sent out as much to the player as to the rest of the team and indeed, to the opposition who were in earshot! This is a rare occurrence on the sub-continent and hence worthy of re-telling.

'Surrendering the me for the we' does not in any way imply that individuals must kill their own ambition. It only suggests an alignment of individual goals with team goals. And if there is a situation where they conflict, team goals must take precedence. It also suggests a culture of co-operation and helping those who are falling behind in performance (and there will always be such people or businesses) to improve and do better. During one of our corporate events the managing director of a large FMCG company told us about a young executive in the firm who was promising but lacked certain skills that would allow him to fulfil his potential. The senior executives worked on him, there was lots of encouragement and some harsh words, but eventually he turned the corner and rose to an impressive position in the organisation. In a 'me' kind of set-up no one would have bothered.

Team Ethics

In the course of our talks, which are now over 300 in number, we've had a sneak peek at most sectors — FMCGs, banks and other financial institutions, pharma, IT, consultancy, BPOs, entertainment, white goods etc. In our opinion, the most challenging in terms of team-building was investment banking. The extreme competitiveness and high degree of confidentiality means that there is almost no trust or sharing within the team. The one thing that probably holds them together is that they all have the same company name on their visiting cards! In one such organisation we did a case study relating to teams. When the discussion started to go contrary to team-building principles, an impromptu question was thrown to the group and a secret vote taken. They were asked if they would commit a foul in the last minute of a football game if they were guaranteed a win, diving in the penalty area to fool the referee, for example. Close to half the group said they would, the outcome clearly more important than the means! Sadly, sport seems to throw up as many situations where taking liberties with the law seems acceptable as it does to others where outstanding and ethical team values are otherwise celebrated.

In another group, a pharma company this time, we were doing a case study on leadership. The situation was a difficult one in which the leader's neck was on the block. The star in the group refused to follow team rules but sacking him would mean that sales would take a big hit. On the other hand, keeping him would set the wrong precedent for the rest. The various groups came up with their solutions, debating what they should do. They didn't want the star but they needed him. The debate heated up and at one point one of the groups suggested that the leader lie to the rest of the group. Suddenly, many others seemed to agree till one gentleman, interestingly an Englishman, got up and said how appalled he was at such a suggestion. This led to a very interesting debate on team ethics which finally ended with the MD, who was merely a spectator till then, sternly making a point that he would never tolerate anything like this.

Nasser Hussain says his county side in Essex, England, were faced with a similar, if less distressing situation. Their top player refused to buy into the team ethic and as the matter dragged on, it began affecting the side. The issue was: do we say goodbye to 1500 runs a year and become a weaker side or put team values first? Eventually, Hussain says, the team had no choice but to say goodbye to the star since retaining him would have meant acceptance of this deviation from acceptable standards.[2]

It is a bit worrisome, though, that increasingly in India we seem to accept expressions like *chalta hai* (anything goes) or *jugaad* — a word instantly recognisable to most Indians but without a suitable English equivalent — where getting things done seems to matter more than how they are done. It is an interesting paradox that India is marrying excellence with processes and yet accepting what, for a great brand, should be unacceptable.

Interdependence

In all businesses as in sport, there are always jobs or roles that are more visible and glamorous. Sales and marketing are like strikers who score goals and create records. Investment consultants are stars, like opening batsmen. HR and admin, like production and distribution, hardly make it to front-page news. In good companies, there is appreciation for the backroom boys who set it all up for the frontline people to achieve their targets. Without top performance from them, the chain would be weak and would affect the team's overall performance adversely.

Hence the importance of the holding midfielder in football. He is the tireless runner whose job is to nip the opposition moves in the bud. He doesn't get onto the score sheet, doesn't make the dramatic goal-line save but stands like a rock and is only really noticed when he is missing. But, like with a good HR manager, he is an integral part of all good teams and among the earliest to be on the team sheet. To that extent he is like a good non-striker who is the key to rotating the strike in a partnership, and ensures that the better player has more of the strike.

In fact, the role of the non-striker was best brought out by Glenn McGrath when he said that five out of Steve Waugh's 32 centuries should be actually claimed by himself because if he had not hung around at the non-striker's end, there was no way Waugh could have scored them! A star can perform only if he is properly supported by the team and that is why setting up a goal is as important as scoring one. If each one tries to score by himself, the team will cease to even function as a team, let alone do well. Mukul Deoras says that one of the tools HUL strongly believed in (from his experience in working there before becoming head of Colgate Palmolive) is listening to the person on the ground and helping him with the right resources. Formerly an avid cricketer himself, he adds, 'Even the best bowler needs the best field placement'.[3]

Indeed, the fielders inside the circle often create the wicket! By cutting off the singles, they force the batsman to play a more dangerous shot and in doing so are effectively setting it up for the bowler to eventually get the wicket. In every good team one arm sets it up for the other to finish. The mid-fielders lay the ball for the striker to score, the batsmen put the runs on the board for the bowlers to bowl freely, and the bowlers keep the runs down so the batsmen have a smaller target to chase. Why, a keeper standing up might force a batsman to play from the crease, which is what the bowler wants! Michael Jordan often went away from the ball and created openings for the others to score.

In the FIFA World Cup of 2006, France tended to play with a lone striker in Thierry Henry. In their quarter final the skilful Spaniards planned to play the off-side trap against him to try and negate him. Aware of that, Henry kept playing closer and closer to the half-line and in doing so, kept drawing the defence further upfield. And when the moment came, Patrick Viera slipped a ball through to the young and lightning-fast Franck Ribery who went through virtually unchallenged through the off-side trap. On the face of it, Ribery scored the goal after a lovely pass from Viera, but it was set up by Henry who was happy to play off the ball and create an opening for someone else.

Holding Teams Together

In creating the 'we', integrating all the diverse groups is critical. Diversity enriches teams by bringing in varied cultures and ways of approaching issues. We see that in the IPL where a Trinidadian sits in the same dressing room as a Sri Lankan and, wonder of wonders, Australians and New Zealanders discuss strategy together. Along with them is the Test star from Bengaluru, but also a young kid from Jharkhand and an inexperienced young man from Vijaywada who might be in awe of the bigger stars. The job of the leader is therefore to ensure that there is free mingling of players to enhance knowledge and also to build team spirit. If the stars are aloof, or worse, disrespectful, it can create discord, even dissent within a side. In diverse teams like in the IPL, or in many global projects, the role of the leader becomes even more critical.

A climate of camaraderie reduces perceived risk in situations when teams are trying something new or innovative. All experiments come with risk attached and the feeling that we are all in it together only helps share the risk. The Sri Lankans demonstrated that at the 1996 cricket World Cup and more recently, Germany showed in the 2006 and 2010 World Cups that if everyone buys into a plan, the results can be thrilling. If either side had paused from time to time to consider the risk, they would not have played with the same freedom.

Marten Pieters, who has now spent some time in India, remembers his early days here and the changes he needed to introduce. 'Earlier decisions were taken on a one-to-one basis (with one's boss). Now it's more team management. Initially, when people said they liked this new way of team management, I said that it wasn't so simple. It's far easier to convince one person (your boss) rather than all your colleagues. Team management is an effort. It sounds a bit slow but once you have decided on it, implementation is far easier. Everybody buys into the decision and then you move very quickly. You spend more time in the beginning but far less in the execution. The earlier system had quicker decisions but needed a lot more fixing in between because it wasn't well thought through.'[4]

Jerry Rao says you can see the 'band of boys' culture in winning teams. Subroto Bagchi calls it 'tribal identity' — common enemy, common and unique language, even common jokes! They have a shared vision and build this tribal identity for themselves. The West Indies cricketers of the late

Seventies and Eighties drew strength from their identity as black cricketers. They talked about making their people proud by their performances. Viv Richards even spoke of knowing his history and of colonisation. Such strong feelings can only exist amidst homogeneity.

So too with Pakistan who displayed a rare sense of togetherness when playing against India, and this enabled them to play fearlessly in matches where fear could well have been the defining emotion. So, as you can see, co-operation and togetherness, irrespective of the binding theme, makes the team more than the sum of its parts and then it's possible to achieve stretch goals by extracting maximum value out of the group.

The key to trust and co-operation within a team is fairness and equality. Steve Waugh says that when he was captain, he treated players 'equally but differently'. Since each person in the team is different and comes with his/her strengths and weaknesses as well as his/her own likes and dislikes, the leader needs to personalise his approach to suit the person. Yet, when it comes to team ethics, discipline, training etc., the rules are the same, irrespective of whether you are the star player or the seniormost team member. Those rules are the non-negotiables!

It is an interesting approach. And so, while it was mandatory for a McGrath or a Warne to be part of the same training sessions as everyone else, they probably got the end they wanted to bowl from or the field they specifically wanted; little things that make the stars; the match-winners feel important. But by insisting that they were on time for say, the team bus, (even the captain Steve Waugh was left behind one day!) they ensured that there was no resentment among the others. It is amazing how much discord little things like unpunctuality can lead to in a team situation.

Stars Can Make or Break a Team

People like Sachin Tendulkar, Rahul Dravid and Anil Kumble, often acknowledged as some of the greatest players the game has seen, are also wonderful examples of players with impeccable team ethic. In fact, Tendulkar often tells the younger players he might be batting or training with, to point out any mistakes he might be making. 'They might hesitate to tell me,' he says 'so it is best I tell them upfront; much better to tell me before I am out rather than after!'

Players with a bad attitude, however talented they may be, can prove to be a burden on the team. While the team needs them as match-winners, they could end up harming the team in the long run by spoiling team dynamics. Shoaib Akhtar was one such player, capable of winning matches for his team with his searing pace but equally capable of ruining team climate by his behaviour.

When the Republic of Ireland qualified for the FIFA World Cup in 2002, their only major star was Manchester United's Roy Keane, a fiery, temperamental character. He complained during training and eventually stormed out of the squad. But far from being demoralised, the team actually came together! The manager, Mick McCarthy, wrote, 'It has taken Keane eight full days to finally do what he tried to do in Saipan last Tuesday night and quit the World Cup, international football and the green jersey. He has tortured and tormented so many of us in the days and nights since then, perhaps even himself. He has walked away from the players he captained…' He went on to say, 'The players are furious that the FAI (Football Association of Ireland) would even consider a return for Roy Keane after everything he said and did. Several of them are adamant that they will go home if Keane is imposed on us…the players won't have him back. They are happy without him.'[5]

As Neeraj Garg says, 'If some people in the team believe that they bring more to the table than others, it results in a fractured team.' Even if people come from different areas, the value that they bring to the team must be on par. The roles they play may be different; some might seem to have more critical ones than others; but every role must be respected. Mutual respect makes collaboration easy and the camaraderie in the team is largely due to this respect that team members have for each other.

Having said that, it is easy for the hugely talented and charismatic players to lapse into behaving like stars. In every team there are those who are more in the limelight than others — not only because of their role but also their personality. A star has the power to make or break a team. If he decides to act like a prima donna, throw his weight around and demand privileges outside of the team's rule book, it is natural that after a while the others will resent him. It's a strange situation, then, when the team needs the star but his teammates don't want him as we saw with Keane. But good teams, with good team-players, rally around the most valuable players so that the rest of the team can draw from their confidence and their knowledge. The Chicago Bulls eventually got there with Michael Jordan, as did the Los Angeles Lakers in the latter part of this decade with Kobe Bryant. The combination of the 'star' and the 'team' can sometimes seem like a tightrope and that is why Nitin Paranjpe is open in his praise of the Australian cricket team which he believes 'successfully marries individual brilliance with organisational consistency'.

We saw a good example of the cult of the individual and the desire to reward the star at the felicitation ceremony of the Indian team after winning the inaugural ICC World Twenty20. While each player got a handsome purse, Yuvraj Singh was given a huge additional sum and an expensive car for hitting six sixes in an over. Admittedly, it was an outstanding performance but there were other players who had played match-winning roles and they could easily have raised the banner of protest. At a time when the team was being celebrated, the cult of the individual was being thrust upon everyone.

Many years earlier, after India had lost a Test match early on the fifth day in Melbourne, the hugely respected former Australian captain and later television broadcaster, Mark Taylor, was walking back to the team hotel when he saw a group of Indian fans celebrating there. When asked what it was they were celebrating, he was told that it was in honour of a Tendulkar century ('best batsman in the world mate...' they went). It didn't seem to matter who had won the match as long as Tendulkar had done well. 'We do things a bit differently here....' Taylor trailed off before getting into the lobby. It was a powerful example of how we can sometimes glorify the individual ahead of the team.

Continuous Improvement

Another indicator of good team climate is the desire to improve continuously – both as individuals and as a team in all aspects of the business. In the world of cricket, there is tremendous appreciation for teams like Sri Lanka and South Africa that came on to the international scene later than the others (especially for South Africa post their return to international cricket) but took very little time to catch up. Teams like Kenya and Bangladesh on the other hand had enough opportunities but lagged behind everyone else.

Teams like Australia, that have been on top, work very hard to stay two steps ahead at all times. The desire to excel can only materialize if the team is willing to stretch and is open to trying out new things. Coaches and captains keep healthy competition alive by keeping the team on its toes. Competition stays healthy when members try to excel by doing the best they can and not with a view to outdo each other at any cost. Good teams make it clear to their members that their real competition is their counterparts from competing teams, not their own teammates. So an opening batsman competes not with the other opener in his team but with openers from the competing team. At one level it may not be bad to spur competition among individual players but it can very quickly lead to a situation where trying to outdo each other becomes paramount, even at the cost of what the team really needs.

At the 2007 World Cup in the West Indies, Adam Gilchrist was having a patchy tournament in the run-up to the final. He says that at the team meeting before the big day he put his hand up and admitted he hadn't done too well but was delighted when the team turned around and told him it didn't matter how much he scored, or his partner Hayden did, individually, as long as they kept giving the team good starts. It was not about Gilchrist or Hayden but about the partnership. It put him in the right frame of mind to demolish the Sri Lankans in the final with an unforgettable innings.

Often we judge a good team as much by who is in it as by who isn't. It adds up. If the quality of people who cannot make the side is excellent, those in it must be even better. And so the quality of the bench is a very good indicator of the quality of the side. And a strong bench competing on performance alone can only add to healthy competition.

The Australians often said that, at their peak, their second eleven was among the top three teams in the world. They like to stick it to the others, the Aussies, and were probably exaggerating. But if you expanded that statement to include the top five teams, the second eleven would comfortably have made it! When the West Indies were on top of the world, part of their aura came from some outstanding fast bowlers who were plying their trade in English county cricket, scaring the daylights out of many teams but with no chance of making their country's first eleven. In such a situation, aware that there are excellent replacements available, those fast bowlers that were in the team could have become insecure. A sure sign of such insecurity is if when you have done well, you don't want a teammate to do too well so that if someone has to be dropped it will be him, not you. When envy starts invading respect, the team is in trouble.

And yet there was great bonhomie among the four quicks and you can see that even today when they speak about each other. Roberts, Holding, Marshall and Garner were quite happy to help each other out, point out faults that might have crept in in the run-up or in the delivery because, as Holding said, 'We were always aware of the fact that we were playing for the West Indies, that people all around the world were looking towards us to do well, and that was always there at the back of our minds'. In essence, it didn't matter who took a wicket as long as the team won. It is a wonderful, almost unparalleled team story.

Team Bonding

The ultimate test that the team is in good shape is the positive body language that creates the buzz in the dressing room. An optimistic attitude can be highly contagious. It manifests itself in the focus on the goal, the eagerness to deliver, in seizing the opportunity and in going for the kill when the opposition is down. Winning teams, Mukul Deoras adds, are also thorough and no one leaves the small details for the other guy to sweat on. The 'can do' attitude is all pervasive, and mates back each other, helping slow performers, co-mentoring and valuing each other's opinions, as we saw with the West Indies fast bowlers. This, according to Sandip Das, is the sign that such teams are secure and apolitical. Trusting, caring and sharing are not merely buzzwords but on display for all to experience. Sometimes we wish these were taught in top management schools as well!

Communication is the final barometer to test team health. Lack of communication, or one-way communication, can spell trouble for any team. Ideally, communication would involve clarity of goals and roles, a respect for the views of all team members, a climate conducive to debate and discussion and finally walking the talk. The last is critical. 'I think there is too much pampering in English cricket, too much of a focus on saying the right things when doing the right things is far more important,' Nasser Hussain said about the England cricket team when he was captain. Nasser believes that it's always better that things are said and no one's left in any doubt. In an interview with Graham Hayday in 2001, he said that this kind of behaviour led to a 'matey' dressing room but he didn't think it would help them get any better.

This 'mateyness' in the dressing room, though not sufficient, is a necessary condition for performance. Winning teams have to be happy teams. And that means that teammates enjoy each other's company and like to spend time with each other even beyond working hours. Success stories and a common goal bind them together and go into making the third requirement for winning teams, collective pride.

One of the signs of happy and successful team-bonding is the pride that individuals have in not only their own success but also in that of their teammates. There is no greater joy for a batsman than to look up at a balcony full of teammates cheering for him on his century. John Wright, former New Zealand captain, insisted that individual success be celebrated collectively when he became coach of the Indian cricket team. Initially, sceptics may see this as forced behaviour, but in the long run it breaks down barriers and inhibitions and becomes second nature. We're all like that. We like people applauding us and when they do, our resistance to applauding for them diminishes!

Collective Pride

Collective pride over the team's success is the best glue any team can wish for. Performing the Hakka, wearing the baggy green or sporting the India jersey are privileges that are priceless. Reliving a successful team climate, recounting experiences and challenges of winning, reinforces the team bond apart from generating confidence. People work not merely for salaries and perks, but for good companies, as more and more organisations are discovering!

A good football club has a following that is loyal through its wins and losses. Loyalty that goes beyond remuneration is what insures companies against poaching from competitors and the key to this insurance is collective pride since not all team wins make all members happy. The Disease of Me is known to make frequent visits even to good teams.

Finally, as Rahul Dravid says, the team is like a pot. Some people put into the pot, others draw from it. Who puts in and who takes out depends on the people as well as the moment. Ultimately, a team that has more people putting in rather than taking out is a happy team, a team more likely to win.

Who is a Team Player?

- Who has a 'greater-than-me' perspective
- Who puts more into the team pot than he takes out
- Who is willing to give up the 'me' for the 'we'
- Who is willing to pass the ball especially when the other guy is in a better position to score
- Who is willing to play in whatever position the team requires him to
- Who gives 100 per cent, every time, under all circumstances
- Who plays by the team rules
- Who is encouraging and is happy to see teammates do well
- Who is proud of belonging to his team
- Who is unafraid to express his opinions

9

Leadership

Inventories can be managed, but people must be led.
—H. Ross Perot

Wasim Akram, Pakistan's most successful fast bowler, with 414 Test wickets and 502 one-day wickets, retired from international cricket in 2003. Even today, when he receives a call from the legendary Imran Khan, Pakistan's most successful cricket captain, Wasim, straightens up and replies with a reverential 'Skipper!' Pakistan, in spite of its immense cricketing talent, won practically nothing of significance before Imran Khan's captaincy and had to wait 17 years after he retired to win the Twenty20 World Championship in 2009. There must have been a reason, because they have never been short of ability. That is why the making of successful leaders, in sports as in business, is something that has always been hotly discussed and debated.

Some people make natural leaders. Others simply fail to inspire. Maybe they believe that those who play international sport should be good enough to understand what to do; or maybe they think that if a player needs to be inspired he is the wrong person to have in the team anyway; or maybe they just cannot understand people! Oddly, we've noticed that the most successful players, more often than not, were not very effective captains while a successful captain like Mike Brearley or a coach like John Buchanan hardly seemed the most qualified for the job. And yet their scholarly ways, quite in contrast with Imran's charisma, seemed to have made a difference.

Often, leadership is perplexing. Winston Churchill, who is remembered as one of the finest leaders during World War II, lost the elections that immediately followed the end of the war. One who made a great wartime leader was rejected as a peacetime manager! Adolf Hitler led, so did the gentle Nelson Mandela.

Reflecting changes in society, cricket, which earlier drew captains from more privileged backgrounds, made way for more middle-class captains. For a long time, England made a distinction between 'Gentlemen' and 'Players'. The former were aristocracy or gentry. Indeed there was a time when that's where you needed to belong to become England captain, and it wasn't till 1952 that a professional or a 'Player', Len Hutton, was appointed the captain. If you needed to earn money from the sport, it was felt, you were probably of the wrong stock! And India, taking its cue from England, had princes as captain on its tours to England before Independence, ahead of cricketers who were more qualified but seemingly, of lower birth. Even Mansur Ali Khan Pataudi, as it turns out, one of India's greatest captains, got the job at 21 because he was seen to have the right background. In later years, Mohammed Azharuddin and Mahendra Singh Dhoni became captains without anyone raising an eyebrow despite their relatively modest backgrounds.

The Role of the Leader

In the course of our sessions, we have often debated whether leadership is something people are born with or indeed, if it can be learnt; whether it is a natural or acquired skill. We believe that there are certain aspects that come along with your DNA or your background. Traditionally in Asia, with its more feudal societies, people needed to look up to a leader as they did in the days gone by to the local chieftain or the prince. In families, fathers were looked up to and were never really one of the boys at home! The era where the leader needed to belong to a certain social class has thankfully gone in India; certainly it has in Indian cricket!

But there are other aspects to leadership (and these are quite a few) that can be understood, acquired and practised. Understanding the role of the captain is also important and while different situations require leaders to display various leadership qualities in different measures, there are certain things that form the core.

I suppose leadership at one time meant muscles; but today it means getting along with people.

—Mahatma Gandhi

A leader's skill is in understanding players and bringing out the best from each player, and in doing so, seeing that the whole adds up to more than the sum of the parts. Michael Holding told us that the reason Clive Lloyd was so respected was that he took the trouble to understand each player, to respect the fact that each person was different. It wasn't a one-size-fits-all style. It was said that Mike Brearley, on the basis of his ability alone, might not have made it to the English team but while being captain, he ensured that his star player Ian Botham was, effectively, worth two players.

Under Sourav Ganguly's captaincy, many young players like Harbhajan Singh and Yuvraj Singh flowered. He empowered them and gave them confidence so that they could become match-winners. In fact Irfan Pathan tells of how he was nervous in his first game and saw the captain throw him the new ball and when he sensed the young man was getting a bit over-awed, ran up to him to tell him how much he believed in him. Pathan said if his captain thought he was good enough, he probably was! At the 1992 World Cup in Australia and New Zealand, Imran Khan had made a public announcement saying he believed that a young man called Inzamam-ul-Huq was the best player of fast bowling. When they got to the semi-final after a scarcely believable, topsy-turvy ride, Inzamam told his captain that he wasn't very keen to play since he wasn't scoring enough runs. Imran told him that he hadn't brought him all the way from Multan to Auckland to drop him. He said he had brought him along because he believed in him and so would play him. The young man played the innings that turned the semi-final around for Pakistan!

In international teams, as in corporates, players make it to the team because they are good enough. A captain or coach, then, needs to make them feel good and happy and create a team climate that supports trust and co-operation. Gautam Gambhir, the Indian opening batsman, felt this need as a player in a team full of batting stars. 'Gary (Kirsten, the coach) told me, he said, how much importance and quality I brought to the side. "You are the one who can anchor the innings, and at the same time you can attack." When you get to know this from a person who has played hundreds of Tests and who is the coach, then you tell yourself, look, even you are equally important. That has made me comfortable. Earlier no one ever told me what importance I brought to the side. I always used to feel, what I am doing in this side anyone else can do. Now I realise I have my own role.'

Similarly, if a player is sent out as a pinch hitter, he must believe that it is being done in the team's best interests, that it is not a ploy to push him into a difficult situation. Also, that if he failed in a difficult situation, it wouldn't be held against him. It is the same with a salesman who is asked to flood a retailer to deny competition shelf space and then finds himself under pressure with his collections.

Therefore, the buzz in the dressing room that spells positivity and energy is largely to do with the climate that the leader creates. Most people in this world don't realise how good they can be and it needs a captain, coach, mentor or boss to encourage wards to challenge themselves all the time, set high goals and grow, as Pathan and many others under Ganguly experienced. John Buchanan calls this 'taking them to places they have never been before'. It's a great line and especially true of players who have come from traditionally weak areas. Who knows how good Mohammad Ashraful of Bangladesh or Steve Tikolo of Kenya would have been in a different environment under a leader who could have taken them to places they had never been before?

Sometimes, leaders choose team members who are clones of themselves. While a leader may seek comfort in having like-minded characters around him, he is effectively killing variety in thought and debate. Heterogeneity and diversity enriches teams and makes up for flaws inherent to the basic DNA of the team. Even in teams that are lucky to have a Sachin Tendulkar in them, there is a need to have a Dravid, a Sehwag and a Yuvraj Singh. Bowlers work in pairs, so do opening batsmen, Gavaskar and Srikanth, for example or, over a longer period, Kumble and Harbhajan. Their differences are what makes them complementary. 'Constructed teams' therefore have a greater chance of being ideal teams and more and more companies are proactively trying to build in diversity into their workforce.

However, captains may not always have the option of a 'constructed' team. They may inherit a lot of dead wood, or simply players who have only done enough to stay in the team and lack the fervour their skippers may be looking for. Or the selectors may not be on the same wavelength as they are, resulting in teams they may not always be comfortable with. Imran, in fact, twice resigned from the captaincy because he couldn't get the team he wanted. But generally, leaders must seek to construct the teams that they believe work the best for the objective they have in mind while, at the same time, encouraging the players they are stuck with to become as good as they can ever be.

What really differentiates a leader from the rest (and hopefully his individuality is the reason he's been chosen for the role) is his vision and ability to look beyond what the others see. He is the captain of the ship who sees the calm beyond the storm. Niall Booker says what a leader needs is perspective — the ability to look at things from a different angle, and if necessary, from someone else's point of view; for example, in the corporate world, the customer's view of a product or service.

The leadership role really begins with the vision, even if it has been largely created by the board of directors or selectors. It's the starting point for the leader, who then communicates it effectively and convincingly to the entire team. It may be as pithy as Manchester United's 'Turning fans into customers' or Nike's 'To bring inspiration and innovation to every athlete in the world' but the leader's job is really to offer a compelling view of the vision to the team. Strategy and goals emerge from this vision and players need to be clear about the goal and the importance of their role, however small, in making it a reality. Some time ago in an ad campaign, ICICI Bank said they would open your account before your coffee grew cold. It was a great line but one that had to be transmitted to the bottom of the chain and bought into by everyone. If the person at the branch didn't buy into the theory, he might have *his* coffee while the customer waited for the account to be opened!

Shane Warne is another who believes very strongly in each player knowing what his role in the side is. After leading the Rajasthan Royals to victory in the first IPL in 2008, completely against the odds, he said, 'Things can change so quickly and you need to adapt. We have some set plans to use depending on conditions, whether we bowl short at the end, whether we bowl full, whether we bowl length, slower balls whatever. You go to a bowler and ask him what he thinks, he might say slower balls and yorkers, so you say okay, switch. Then the players know the field for that. The most important thing is to let the players know what their role is, what they are expected to do. That's where we had an advantage last year. We were very well prepared and we gave everyone a role and nickname. Graeme Smith was the "Rock at the Top". He batted with Swapnil Asnodkar who was the "Goa Cannon" — go and hit them. We had all these names that the guys loved. A lot of other teams just go out and play and they expect them [the players] to know and they can be dictated to by scoreboard pressure.'[1]

It is true though that sometimes a player might perceive his role to be insignificant, even unpopular, but if the captain communicates to him that it is critical, he will still do a very effective job of it. It's the captain's job, then, to draw the line between being popular or otherwise, and being effective. Nasser Hussain, who did so well for England as a leader, says

'I'd be wary of anyone who's a popular captain because it means the players are getting their own way all the time and getting to do the things they want to do and sometimes you want them to do things they really don't want to do. That's why you have to keep with them so they respect you. You need to keep in mind that you're one of them, and not take yourself too seriously and become some kind of superior being in the dressing room. But you have to get the balance between being one of them and also making sure that when you speak, they listen.'[2]

Hussain was to experience this situation when England came to India under him in 2002 and ran into Sachin Tendulkar in top form. Unable to work out a way of getting him out, they decided to frustrate him by bowling a largely negative outside the leg stump line. The man assigned to do the job was Ashley Giles, a workmanlike spinner who kept things tight. For the next eleven overs he bowled outside the leg stump to Tendulkar, a tactic that drew much criticism. But it did keep Tendulkar quiet and ended up frustrating him. 'If you can't bowl him out, bore him out,' the critics said, but as Hussain suggested afterwards, it was a better option than letting Tendulkar get a century! It was a boring job for Giles to do and the key lay in the captain's communication of its importance. If a player knows his role and implements it well, a seemingly small role can become important. Or, at the very least, raise a player's self-esteem as we saw with Gambhir.

There are times when the team is doing well enough and there are no external threats to keep it on its toes. Or if the side is a chronic winner — way ahead of competition —

like the Australian cricket team was all through the Nineties and early 2000s. Such teams need to be challenged to keep their hunger intact. Many companies too find their growth rate steadying at a comfortable level, with no perceived need to do anything dramatically different. They face the risk of becoming complacent. Injecting some positive turbulence in teams shakes them up and gets them going.

Positive turbulence is a lovely expression for it means that the leadership is alive to the need of getting ready for what the future might throw up, and getting ready for it in advance. It means you are creating disturbance in the side with a view to benefiting everyone. In the mid-Nineties Sri Lanka were a talented side just finding their way in the world. They had players of great skill but not all of them were necessarily athletic enough. That could, in times to come, become an obstacle and so when a new coach arrived, he insisted the team follow a fairly rigorous fitness regimen. It rubbed off on everyone and the new generation Sri Lankan cricketer, a Malinga or a Sangakkara, is possessed of a very different shape from those that took the field earlier. Had the turbulence not been created on time, Sri Lanka may not have become the side that was respected around the world and which reached the World Cup final in 2007.

Who Makes a Good Leader

History judges leaders by the quality of the decisions they take. The outcome may not always be beneficial but the boldness and intent behind the decision are what matter. Whether in war, business or sport, decision-making is an integral part of leadership. And those who dilly-dally or fail to take a call are remembered as weak and ineffective leaders. A delay in declaring the innings for example, or a wrong choice of bowler, or a wrong call taken after winning the toss are things that could decide the course of the match, and often those who choose wisely are the ones that become successful. Australia played Pakistan in the 2009-10 series and had a wonderful opportunity to beat the world champions at home. They had Australia on the ropes with eight wickets down and very few runs in the bank. Instead of going in for the kill, captain Mohammed Yousuf suddenly went defensive, placing fielders on the boundary line and waiting for the batsmen to make a mistake. By the time they did, too many runs had been scored and the game was lost. Yousuf was weighed down by leadership rather than buoyed by it!

This is an important point to study before appointing leaders. Are they likely to be weighed down by leadership or buoyed by it? Does their own performance dip due to the additional pressure, as might have happened with Sachin Tendulkar, or does their personality bloom as it did with Sourav Ganguly? Some people enjoy being leaders, you can see that in their body language, others are inherently private people happy to contribute but who find it a burden to take on any responsibility beyond that which they can carry out.

Madhabi Puri-Buch, former MD and CEO, ICICI Securities believes that there are two kinds of leaders: those who believe that 'HR stuff' is an interruption of work, and those that believe that it is the most important part of the leader's work. This difference in approach is what, she believes, determines whether the leader flowers or gets bogged down.[3]

It is said that a boardroom where you can hear a single voice is not a very vibrant place. A leader has to be a 'hear-a-holic' — with open ears and an open mind since the best ideas can sometimes come from where you least expect them. They could come from one of the 'reserves'; he has little to do, has no pressure at all and might spot something that has escaped more anxious eyes. He too must be heard. And yet, the final decision has to be the leader's alone. Steve Waugh, in an interview, spoke of the time he had just become captain of Australia: 'As captain, you are in charge and you are responsible for what happens on the field. In a way I was very inexperienced and in that pressure-cooker situation you don't know how you will cope. Initially, I didn't follow my instincts, took advice from too many people. You need to take advice but finally it has to be your own decision. You can't ask people how to run your business — you have to work it out for yourself.'

New leaders, in particular, tend to ask people around them for their view but rarely is a decision arrived at by consensus. It's also not possible or even desirable for leaders to make everyone happy in the final outcome. Leaders who try to do that rarely achieve success. It requires courage and conviction to take decisions and even more to stand by them. A former Indian cricket captain who tried to involve too many people in deciding strategy also refused to hold himself accountable when he realised that an error in judgement had occurred. Eventually, the buck rests with the leader irrespective of whether the call taken was the right one or not and irrespective of all those who were involved. As Ian Chappell says, 'The Ws and Ls (wins and losses) go against your name.'

A captain can never think 'what if' — what if he had taken another decision, for example, what if he had placed another man in the slips, what if he had hiked his advertising budget, what if he had implemented specific new software …. If you have put the opposition in, you have to believe you will win a game even if you don't get instant results; have to believe in your decision, have to keep looking ahead however steep and unlikely the outcome.

It was something Shane Warne instilled in his young players during the dramatic ride to victory for the Rajasthan Royals in the inaugural IPL (as we read briefly in Chapter Two). His mantra to his players was to be positive at all times. Never worry about the situation you are in because that is already upon you, he told them. Instead, ask yourself how you can win from here. Having said that, he then empowered young players to play on the big stage, often drawing performances out of them that they probably didn't think they were capable of themselves! It is an important leadership trait: to believe in your players and give them confidence, for a team that is not empowered is a timid team.

Imran Khan believes that optimism is a key quality that a leader must possess. He recalled that halfway during the 1992 World Cup, when Pakistan's chances of reaching the final stages were minimal, Intikhab Alam, who was the team manager at the time, came to Imran to find out his opinion on flight arrangements for the team to fly back home. Imran was surprised and promptly told Intikhab to come back when they actually lost. The rest, as they say, is history.

Sanjay Manjrekar, who had a wonderful series in Pakistan in 1989, and has watched a lot of cricket there, said, 'I never once saw Imran Khan looking towards the stands, or looking elsewhere, He was constantly at us, even if it was a boring Test match. He was always at us … also, I think not allowing the slightest negativity to creep in … within himself and the rest of the team. Rameez Raja told me how he never ever talked about how good the opposition batsman was. He always talked about how "we" can do it. Even if deep down he knew that the opposition was better, he never let his teammates feel that way.' In fact a large number of the corporate leaders we spoke to for this book emphasised the importance of this. The 'can-do' attitude is a defining one.

A leader would be particularly disadvantaged if he was lacking in communication skills. This is not as much to do with fluency and glibness as it is to do with coming through as genuine, and the ability to connect with the heterogenous people who sometimes constitute a team. It's about reaching out to those who are not doing so well. It's about trusting the team and being seen as someone who can be trusted.

When he appeared on our show *Masterstrokes* on CNBC, Sourav Ganguly said that even if he got it wrong five times out of ten, the team trusted him and believed that he made mistakes while trying to do his best for the team. No wonder he was credited with changing the fortunes of the team as captain! It is a wonderful position for the leader to reach, and highlights why generating trust is one of the fundamental tenets of leadership.

However, the extent of communication, like good spices in a curry, needs to be just right! Ian Chappell believes that if captains over-communicate, it may prove ineffective, and so he left speech-making for the big and important occasions when it would have the desired impact. E.A.S. Prasanna too remembers Tiger Pataudi as being a captain of few words. But a nod or mere shake of the head from Tiger was enough, says Prasanna.

Tiger Pataudi, with his royal lineage and Oxford education, was much younger than, and socially, quite far removed from, many of the other players from the team. Tiger was made captain of India at the young age of 21. In fact he captained in 41 of the 46 Tests that he played. Tiger could never have been one of the boys as Dhoni is today. And yet his charisma, quite like Imran Khan's, made him a respected captain. By contrast, Western teams are far more egalitarian. Mukul Deoras sums it up by saying, 'Western leaders depend more on clarity of two-way communication and implicit delegation. Eastern leadership is perhaps a lot more feudal. They depend on clarity of instruction and alignment.'[4]

'Many companies in India are promoter-owned which brings a very strong personal leadership where, typically, the thinking and the main decision-making is done at the very top and the rest is more or less execution. Even if it's at a very high level, it's still execution. There is a very well-defined area of authority and outside of that you go back to the boss. In our system (which is far more egalitarian), you come back to the team,' observes Marten Pieters.[5]

Like the Indian vs. expat issue, the leader from inside vs. the outsider issue has also been discussed at great length. Mukul Deoras believes that an outsider is important if we believe that the team is incapable of thinking outside its set pattern and/or needs competencies which are not available within the team. Hence the reason for looking at overseas coaches, as for example, in Indian cricket.

Sandip Das has an interesting take on this which seems to justify Ian Chappell's thinking. He says, 'Most mothers complain that their children suffer from "mother deafness" because they are constantly chiding their children and the kids do not seem to respond … then fathers say the same thing and suddenly things happen. CEOs feel similarly about CEO deafness. You could be saying wonderful new things to your people and the response could be frustratingly lukewarm. Yet one fine day, you get a CEO of another company to come in to talk to your people. When he leaves, they will rave about the wonderful things he said, although you might have been saying them for years inside the company. So, occasionally it helps to get that little intervention from outside, for changes and impact. It is a symptom of freshness, new perspective and arguably, more perceived objectivity.'[6]

Tiger Tyagarajan, who has spent many years with GE, known as a training ground for so many global leaders, says that GE has a systematic process of grooming future leaders and when these leaders do take over, their team accepts them more easily. It is almost expected that they take over. Australia tend to do that and when one captain retires, the identity of his successor is rarely a mystery. The continuity helps. Australia had only four captains between 1985 and 2010, whereas Pakistan might have gone through those many in a few months! Tiger believes that outside leaders need to be parachuted in only to organisations where there is no process in place or 'when there is no credit given to mentors or there is a lack of self-confidence and security among current leaders who then don't hire people better than them and who could take their job.'[7]

True leaders like challenges so that they can prove themselves in tough situations. So although a crisis or change or downturn might find the team in turmoil, leaders are willing to give it a go as a personal challenge. Some coaches would rather coach a Sri Lanka or a New Zealand, which are good but have a lot more scope for improvement, than a team like Australia that was on top for a while. Some others might believe that *staying* on top is almost as difficult a challenge. It is an interesting question for leaders to ask themselves. Which team would you rather lead? A team that's been number one for ten years or another that is number six, has limited resources, but has the potential to make it big?

Inevitably all attention on the field drifts towards the leader. Teams that are down look to him for direction and would rather see a calm captain than one who is seen to be chewing his nails or gesturing all over the place. Mark Taylor was known for his unflappable nature and it was impossible to know by watching him whether his team was struggling or cruising. So too with Mahendra Singh Dhoni. The opposition should be led to believe that the leader might still have a few aces up his sleeve and, certainly, that he isn't going to give up easily.

It is appropriate therefore that Ian Chappell talks about the need for a captain to even out his own emotions whatever his own performance. 'Don't yell on the field,' he says, 'because that sends out a signal to the opposition.' A captain's own performance can be an irritant to the job unless that can be effectively separated from leadership. Some years ago, when still captain of India, Sourav Ganguly said he had told Rahul Dravid, who he thought would be India's next captain, about the importance of taking decisions as captain whether or not he is getting runs. 'If you mix up the two roles you are in trouble,' he said.

An optimistic leader, one who displays confident body language can also be the glue for a team in a crisis. Teams rally around such leaders. John Buchanan's theory of the coach being redundant may hold for a winning team but we believe that a team in trouble must have a visibly hands-on leader, like Rudy Giuliani, the mayor of New York, was during 9/11. Or it must have a leader who possesses the quality of leadership that Bharat Puri displayed during the 'worms in chocolate' affair. When you have inspirational leaders taking on a situation, players can end up playing for the captain — which is not a bad thing really.

When Leaders are Tested

Teams sometimes go into a losing streak and end up getting white-washed in the series. Often, this is not due to poor performance alone but because morale has taken a beating as well. Teams end up taking the field convinced they cannot win, look around at each other and wonder which of them is going to be a match-winner. At such times matches tend to be lost before they actually are. But then, good players don't get bad overnight, which explains the cliché: class is permanent, form is temporary. The most natural reaction of a leader would be to focus on improving the performance but this is hardly likely without morale being boosted. Often it is a re-injection of self-belief that brings the team back on track.

Sometimes leaders need to take tough calls like giving negative feedback or dropping a player. Such decisions, however painful, can neither be avoided nor delayed. Rahul Dravid faced public outcry when, as captain in Pakistan, he declared the innings with Tendulkar not out on 194. But that was a decision that needed to be taken if the team was to win. It needs a tough captain to take tough decisions, to put the team ahead of an individual landmark. Eventually, the leader who puts the team first tends to be respected.

We saw that twice during Test matches in England. The first was in 1997 at Manchester, when the Australian captain Mark Taylor made a seemingly puzzling decision. The conditions were overcast, the pitch was green and it was a toss crying to be won so that the opposition could be asked to bat first. However, Taylor knew that on that surface, spinners would come into the game on day four and five, and so, to allow Shane Warne to bowl in the fourth innings and try and win Australia the Test, they needed to bat first. Steve Waugh writes, 'when Tubby (Taylor) returned and announced he had won the toss and elected to bat, disbelief swept the room. On the surface his decision appeared foolhardy and a massive gamble but he had backed his gut ... A captain needs to see the bigger picture.'

And in the 2002 Test series between India and England, India went to Leeds one down with two games to play. It was a blustery day, the pitch was a touch damp, rain was in the air, again a win–toss–bowl-first pitch. But India's captain Sourav Ganguly backed his side to combat the conditions and batted first. It was a vote of confidence in the team and they rallied to the call. Once the conditions were conquered, runs were made quite freely and India drew the series.

So, as you can see, leaders need to take tough decisions during tough times. During the 2008-09 recession, companies floundered. Executives who were used to luxuries during boom times, were suddenly asked to cut back costs, forgo bonuses, even move into smaller houses. It's difficult to ask people for more while giving less. One way of getting around things is for the leader to set the example. Niall Booker at HSBC said, 'If you are asking people to cut back, you need to be seen to do the same. I got rid of the Mercedes and had a Honda Accord as the company car in India. People need to trust you.' In a similar vein, Barry Richards said of Ian Chappell, 'He never asked people to do something he wouldn't do himself. He didn't believe in a nightwatchman and wanted a batsman to go out himself. But then he did the same when it was his turn'

There is a feeling that Indian managers generally shy away from giving timely and honest feedback. This is because Indians treat feedback as criticism and don't take it as constructive feedback that will help them improve. Indians are also people-oriented, often putting people ahead of the task. This shows in the way we are so poor with constructive culling, often letting non-performers continue well beyond their sell-by date. It helps nobody, because a leader's skill lies as much in picking a player at the right time as in letting him go at the required moment. But because we are sentimental people we tend to hang on to our good-byes and while the intent can be noble at a personal level, it is not a great teambuilding tactic, for there is a fear of accumulating non-performing people assets.

A. S. Ramchander, Executive Director at Castrol India at one time, told us, 'Within an organisation, honesty in giving feedback is often avoided in order to be polite. The evaluator [the one giving feedback] will have credibility only if he is honest. Yet specifics are missed out and the once-a-year performance appraisal confuses the juniors.'[8]

However, Indian managers seem to have an inherent advantage in managing uncertainty as well as diversity. As Jerry Rao puts it, 'Indians are used to cultural diversity from a young age. Since our infrastructure is so bad, when things go wrong, they know how to improvise. They develop the smarts that, say, people working in Singapore, where everything works like clockwork, don't develop. We also have an irrational government that takes abrupt policy decisions that could upset your cost calculation and competitive advantage. Such abrupt decision-making is required in hi-tech industries as well, though not due to the external environment. One learns to adapt and put multiple bets on the possible outcomes.

Indians are used to dealing with labour unions who can have a completely different agenda. It helps you realise that there could be another point of view.'9

This was amply demonstrated by Lalit Modi when, in a span of a mere three weeks, he successfully moved the second IPL tournament to South Africa after the Central government expressed its inability to guarantee sufficient security-cover for the players in the wake of elections being announced at around the same time as the IPL. To move a tournament of such magnitude, involving such complicated logistics and international participation at such short notice says a lot about Lalit Modi's guts as well as his decision-making. To many it would have seemed an impossible move but as always, in difficulty there lurks an opportunity. By producing an impeccable IPL 2, Modi produced a global Indian brand that may not have been possible had it remained in India. One of the lessons there, as mentioned earlier in this chapter, was that in times of crisis, you need a hands-on leader who is looking beyond apparent difficulties.

The Best Player Need not Make the Best Captain

Thank God that Imran Khan did not suffer from insecurity, or else the cricketing world would have missed players like Wasim Akram and Waqar Younis. Because Imran always put Pakistan first, and was very secure himself, he didn't mind picking young players who, in a few years, would actually become better than him, for his skills would decline with age. But he also believed in leading from the front and so, when his fast-bowling skills had significantly declined during the World Cup campaign of 1992, he moved up to number three in the batting order. The captain was making a statement there.

What starts early in life with the best student in class being made the class monitor continues till much later with the best salesman being made sales manager or the star batsman becoming captain. The law of natural progression is followed the world over, in spite of it being proved wrong over and over again. Star performers are supreme individualists, totally focused on themselves and their craft. In a sense, their obsession with themselves is what defines their genius.

A leader, on the other hand, needs to think beyond himself and ahead of everyone else. He needs to relate to people whose talent does not match his own, and needs to spend time with players who are not performing as well as him. And in doing so, answer for himself the question that every leader must: Do I spend more time with people who are in form and delivering or do I spend more time with under-performers who need some hand-holding?

Indeed, one reason outstanding talents don't always make the best leaders is that they tend to weigh everyone in the same scales they weigh themselves in and so, sometimes are unable to understand the limited capability, even the insecurity, of another player. As one international player said to us about his captain, 'Has he ever known what it is to go to bed wondering if he will make the team the next day?' In fact Sachin Tendulkar admitted to us in the interview we did with him that his fast bowler Javagal Srinath told him that he tended to measure people in the way he measured himself.

Understanding the person, therefore, is critical because you still need him on the team and need to get the best out of him.

Michael Holding, as we have seen, said something similar when we asked him about his captain Clive Lloyd. There was a feeling that you didn't really need to do much with that great West Indies side since everyone knew their role and they were the most awesome bunch of players to take the field. (In years to come, New Zealander Chris Cairns would say that his mother could captain Australia!) But as Holding said, 'Lloydy took the trouble to understand that we were all different and because he respected us, we respected him.'

The other reason the best performer need not make the best leader, therefore, is that leadership requires a whole new set of skills. An outstanding software programmer, for example, caught up in the daily affair with his machine, might never learn to handle people; a very good shop floor manager might not possess the communication skills to lead a less homogeneous group. Understanding that the qualities that brought you so far are not the ones that will necessarily take you forward is an adjustment that many fail to make. And so teams might be better off looking at less-gifted individuals if indeed they possess the ability to bring the best out of the team.

The need to have both skills — being a performer and being able to understand the capability of others — is therefore a combination that few possess, for, as Madhabi Puri-Buch told us, 'The leader must also come with impeccable credentials. Today's youngsters, in particular, will not respect a leader if he/she is not a performer in his/her own right.' Her philosophy is that a leader can command respect only if he is able to say, 'If you can't do it, I will.'[10]

Genius also has a twin brother in ego, and success only strengthens the bond between the siblings. Saugata Gupta feels that greed and a lack of humility are the two main reasons why leaders fall. 'Sometimes, leaders get caught up in pet projects. You should be able to judge things from a distance. Often, there aren't people who will tell the leader that he is wrong. It is lonely at the top.'

Leaders Come with a Shelf-Life

While discussing leadership issues we often talk about different situations needing, almost demanding, different kinds of leaders. Wartime generals are required for inspired action, for taking the bull by the horns. Peacetime managers are brought in when you need to sustain a campaign. Neither of those skills is superior — as seen by the case of Winston Churchill who was rejected by the British electorate when the need to rebuild, after the euphoria of the victory in the war, became paramount.

Post the match-fixing issue at the turn of the century, Indian cricket needed a flamboyant, inspirational leader, not just to carry the team along but to convince the fans that they were out there doing their best. Sourav Ganguly was the right man and he was wonderful in transforming India from a defensive, uncertain side, especially overseas, into one that could win anywhere. By doing that he brought the people back into the game and towards supporting the national side. In fact, you could say cricket in India recovered almost too quickly from that match-fixing affair!

By 2005, India were respected around the world but Ganguly's own form was taking a dip and there was a feeling he might be a touch insecure. When the time came for a change, India found an outstanding peacetime manager in Rahul Dravid whose style was rather more low-key. And so, without making headlines for his leadership, he took India to victory in the West Indies in 2006, for the first time in 35 years, and in England in 2007, for the first time in 21 years. Ganguly and Dravid were the right people at the right time; one a wartime leader, the other a peacetime manager.

As indeed were Anil Kumble and Mahendra Singh Dhoni. Kumble, with his dignity and stature, and compulsive work ethic, was the right man for a potentially draining tour of Australia in 2008, and the small-town Dhoni just about perfect to lead new India and its aspirations which he could understand better than anyone else.

This sense of timing is critical in industry as well, as we have seen in the next generation of Bajajs and as we have almost certainly seen in the trend-setting Ambanis. Dhirubhai was the pioneer, starting small, recognising opportunity, and building the company. But as India changed and began taking its place in the world, Reliance found that Mukesh Ambani, with his global outlook and ambition was the man for the occasion. Maybe it is purely an academic issue whether both father and son would have done equally well if the roles, and timing, were reversed but Reliance certainly benefitted enormously from having the right people leading it at the right time.

Another example that illustrates this quite vividly was Australia's resurgence in the late Eighties. In the mid-Eighties, plagued by the mistrust that arose between the former Packer players and those that backed the establishment, and grievously injured by the rebel tours to South Africa, Australia had hit rock bottom in the world of cricket. Much to their discomfiture they were even being beaten by their little cousin, New Zealand. And their captain, Kim Hughes, had tearfully resigned the captaincy.

Almost by default then, the mantle was delivered to a tough, stubborn back-room boy called Allan Border. With coach Bob Simpson, and with a lot of help from the selectors (the importance of everyone in the management sticking together?) Border and Australia decided to rebuild on the 'attitude first' principle. They selected mentally-tough, proud cricketers, sometimes ahead of more gifted players who may not have had the right attitude. You could see that in the selection of people like Steve Waugh, and David Boon who once, famously, asked for an injury to be stitched up on the field rather than leaving it and giving away a psychological advantage.

Border's philosophy in Test cricket was, understandably, geared towards not losing for he had seen enough of it. Australia battled hard, fielded brilliantly but were gritty rather than flair cricketers. By and by, the victories started to arrive. The World Cup of 1987 and the Ashes in 1989 had been important landmarks but Australia still couldn't beat the West Indies. Border had been part of too many losing campaigns against them.

By 1993-94, it became apparent that Border was coming to the end of his career. The team was fairly stable now but the big win against the West Indies was still eluding them. Australia's selectors then took the tough call and decided that Mark Taylor would replace Allan Border as captain on his retirement. Taylor was as different from Border as possible. He had always been captain of his side, enjoyed it and always looked to win. It helped him that he had inherited a fairly stable side but the mindset still needed to change. With Taylor's forward-looking, aggressive approach, Australia beat the West Indies for the first time in the Caribbean in 1995.

With both Border and Taylor, and Ganguly and Dravid, it was the right man in charge at the right time. Had the order been reversed, Taylor in the mid-Eighties and Border thereafter, Australia may not have been as well served.

In management too, leaders who steer companies out of tight situations with prudent controls and tight spending, could find it difficult to lead the ship when giant investments fuelled by optimism are the need of the hour. You need grit in one situation and vision in another. You need someone to count the paise in one situation and someone to invest the big rupees in another.

Not surprisingly, therefore, leaders have a shelf-life too. Ian Chappell thinks there is a voice inside that tells you when it is time to go. There comes a time when the speeches seem tired, the new ideas seem familiar and the tricks become repetitive. Or sometimes, pressure takes its toll and the leader can feel spent; that could start affecting his performance as a player. But there is no formula for determining shelf-life. Jose Mourinho was thought good enough for two years at Chelsea but Alex Ferguson seems to go on and on for Manchester United. Ganguly did the job for five years while Dravid thought his time had come in two. It is something that those that appoint leaders need to keep an eye out for. That is why, as with players, leaders need to be picked and culled at the right time.

Who is a Good Leader?

- Makes the team add up to more than the sum of the parts
- Has vision and communicates to inspire
- Manages team climate
- Is trusted and respected
- Backs the team at all times
- Is approachable and understands the team
- Empowers the team, creates more leaders
- Takes them to places they have never been before
- Is open, flexible, honest and a hear-a-holic
- Is positive, optimistic
- Is courageous in decision-making; always works in the interest of the team

- Is secure, willing to surround himself with people better than himself
- Can accept responsibility and give credit
- Serves as team glue

10

Challenges in Today's World

You can't put a limit on anything. The more you dream, the farther you get.

—Michael Phelps

Much has changed in the 25 years during which we have followed both sport and business. It's been quite a time. There has probably been more change in the last 20 years than in the last century. For India in particular, these have been the growing-up years. Businesses have had to reinvent themselves and, with times changing, so have managers. The scale of business has grown beyond anything that we could have ever imagined, from the time you booked a trunk call and waited, sometimes days, for it to come through, or splurged on a PP (particular person) call to carrying your office in your pocket with your cell phone!

A New Generation

Technology has altered the traditional price-demand equation. Knowledge, not experience, is the new driver and a generation that lived by constraints has been replaced by one that is led by its dreams. It is a critical aspect of this all-encompassing change. Older values like living within one's means, humility and conformity, no longer appeal to the new generation to whom credit and high-flying seem the only way to live.

New-age cricketers too, in keeping with the times, are more flamboyant, market-savvy and unconventional in their approach. The emergence of the Twenty20 format perhaps demands this kind of approach. There is as much happening around the game as in it, and it's becoming increasingly challenging for players not to get distracted from the game. There is a 'Beckham Effect' at play. David Beckham's potential in marketing football jerseys was often just as important as his trademark cross from the right. And so, marketability joins skill in the factors that determine value.

The new consumer, the new sportsman as also the young workforce is a strange and unfamiliar animal, and managers are having to deal with a whole new set of challenges. What it also means is that much of what the forty-plus managers learnt at B-school is no longer valid and therefore of not much use in day-to-day life. They are having to unlearn and learn again, or risk falling behind. Indeed, understanding young cricketers is not too different from understanding young managers. Their expectations are high and grit isn't always fashionable! What the forty-plus manager thought was wrong could well be the new right.

The biggest change has been that people are now being recognised as a company's true assets. It is now possible to buy technology, R&D, know-how, and get easy access to capital, making the quality of people a company hires the only true differentiator. The services sector has grown much more in comparison to others, making the selection of employees even more critical. Now, more than ever before, every business is a people's business. India has no dearth of talent but talent is not much use without the right work ethic, and hugely-talented people can actually be a burden if they can't fit into teams. Mergers and acquisitions alter the DNA of an organisation and can result in Us-and-Them situations that leave teams fractured. With constant churning, companies and teams are asking themselves 'Who are we?' Little mini-companies can be formed in larger companies and you can be left with islands of different cultures!

In many of the sessions we conduct we find people saying that the team is hugely talented but they have issues with team spirit. Either people work in silos or the culture is very individualistic. Sadly, teamwork is not taught at most business schools today. There is a lot of group work involved but we were told by a batch mate at our IIM-A silver jubilee reunion that that sense of camaraderie that once existed no longer does in today's very driven generation and that people even feign illness in order to bunk group work so that they can study by themselves. Extreme drive, that leads to selfishness, makes one wonder: winning is important, but at what cost? Will opportunity and competition lead to the cult of the individual?

While a knowledgeable and vibrant young generation is the need of the day, having overly-driven early achievers in the team can present problems to older managers as well as to other colleagues with average performances. Their sky-high salaries and even more attractive perks (once the recession is forgotten, it's likely to be the same old story) create monster-like egos that are a leader's nightmare. Sports, like finance and investment banking, is full of unfortunate stories about sudden success, the trappings of money and fame, followed by early burn-out.

When Twenty20 cricket began, everyone believed it would be a young man's game. While speed and risk-taking are known to be the preserve of youth, three IPL seasons later, many from the older guard who adapted to the new format have been found to be more consistent and reliable compared to the fiery but inconsistent youngsters. This is often attributed to the many distractions like big money (at the very start of their careers for many players) that the IPL brought with it. Maybe Sachin Tendulkar should run a course on how to keep your feet on the ground and your focus on your work. And maybe this must be made compulsory for all the young managers at BPOs as well.

On the other hand, today's generation is very smart, technologically savvy and very clued into global developments. Occasionally, we have found companies unable to keep up with the ambition and drive of this generation. It reminds us of Richard Hadlee or Brian Lara who must have experienced this kind of frustration, having belonged to teams that didn't do justice to their talent. It can be a revelation to some that companies need to keep pace with the ambitions of their employees.

A New India

Globalisation has brought with it new standards in best practices and processes. Indian managers are now in great demand globally. While expat managers have to learn to deal with the chaos and uncertainty that comes with working in India, Indians have had to learn to work in diverse teams. Workers from research and technology who have not had to deal with people are now suddenly finding themselves in leadership positions. It's not easy for them to adapt. Indian cricketers, hockey players and sportsmen from other disciplines as well have grown up in a system that glorifies flair and style. From so many foreign coaches and proximity to other international players who put process above individual style, a whole lot of things need to be learnt.

India has suddenly become a very important market for most multi-nationals. India's large domestic demand at least partially shielded the market during the recent recession. A number of companies have major manufacturing facilities here. The expectations from headquarters, apart from the mind-boggling consumer base that has always caught the imagination of the Western world, translates into targets which managers initially find overwhelming. These also demand working in newer geographies, newer ways of doing business and an approach that requires each person to be proactive and think of himself as a decisionmaker. This is a big change for those who have been used to getting instructions from their bosses in strongly hierarchical companies. All the IT companies we interacted with emphasised the growing need for their employees to change their mindset from being mere software-or hardware-providers to becoming customer-centric integrated solutions-providers. This approach would require complete ownership of the problem as well as the solution.

Opportunities to scale up and diversify are available in plenty to most sectors. IT companies, pharma MNCs and BPOs are all aware that only the sky is the limit. Executives without vision are finding these figures mind-boggling and unreal while leaders are making them aware of the largeness of the pie. While the opportunity is huge, it comes with the realisation that winning today does not necessarily translate into winning tomorrow since tomorrow could be so vastly different from what today is. It is making corporate leaders think about getting their organisations future-ready in terms of infrastructure, processes and people. The pressure to remain relevant and contemporary in a fast-changing world is taking a toll on managers, adding to the already high levels of attrition.

Companies that spend significant sums on training can do so confidently only if people stay with the organisation. Companies invest not only in employees but also JV partners, associates, dealers and distributors, suppliers and BPOs managing the back-office. And they also expect all these stakeholders to keep pace with them since growth can only happen if the approach is inclusive. Sport too has become a business with many, diverse stakeholders. Television networks and production houses, advertisers and media houses, players and agents, teamowners and sponsors — apart from audiences watching on the ground or on television. All of them need to be managed, which in itself is a drastic change from how things used to be.

Changing Team Dynamics

Globalisation has also meant dealing with new concepts in team dynamics. Dealing with diversity requires a finer sensibility and a greater understanding of cultures that are almost alien. The communication challenge is not merely about language but also about norms and tradition. Full marks, therefore to Shane Warne a hardcore Aussie who could not only communicate with his largely non-English speaking Rajasthan Royals team but also reach out to the young Indian kids in the team who surely would have been in awe of him and too tongue-tied to ask him about anything at all. Maybe there is a very interesting case study there for expat managers in India, as we found out ourselves when the head of a multinational bank asked us if we could introduce him to Greg Chappell. 'I think I could talk to him about doing business in India,' he said with a smile.

Not only are teams heterogeneous these days, but also multi-locational and temporary. Outsourcing means that there's a good chance that you may never come face-to-face with your overseas colleagues. And then, like in projects, you join a new team every once in a while. Building affinity in such teams, getting them to be part of a common vision, is an enormous challenge. Building loyalty in the IPL teams as well as among their fans is probably the biggest task before the IPL franchises. Playing alongside somebody one day and against him the very next week, and being equally committed to both, couldn't be easy on players either.

In the absence of strong identification with your team, and this can so easily happen, confidentiality of company information would naturally be a matter of concern. Anyway, with high levels of people movement, competitors would be keen to employ people from rival firms to get easy access to their strategies. Wouldn't it be tempting to know from a Gambhir the strengths and weaknesses of a Dhoni?

A dynamic environment comes with an 'adapt or perish' rider, something we see in sport every day. Self-growth and the effort to remain relevant and contemporary, and yet have an eye on the future, need to be given as much priority as the day-to-day demands at the workplace. As we discussed earlier, personal obsolescence is a real threat and those who live in denial are bound to fall behind. Winning tomorrow is as important as winning today. In teams too, the trick is in developing young players around the older players who are established but will retire.

We have also seen that scale has stopped providing the edge in many sectors. Smaller players who are nimble-footed, hungrier and willing to go the extra mile are coming up with innovations that are shaking up the markets. A company like Mankind, a more recent entrant to the pharmaceutical industry, came up with a rather aggressive pricing strategy and an unusual thrust on rural and semi-rural markets, and forced giants from the industry to rethink their strategies. Innovations like cricket's latest shot, the 'Dilscoop', introduced and perfected by Tilakaratne Dilshan, give the innovator a lead over competition until everyone else figures it out. Whether in credit cards or mobile phone services or insurance, somebody introduces a new feature and the rest of the players are forced to follow suit. It's a catching-up game that gives the first mover a small and sometimes temporary advantage. When the innovator is a small and relatively new player, the firmly-entrenched players tend to ignore him for a while but this can prove expensive. By the time an Ajantha Mendis has been acknowledged and figured out, the match has already been conceded. We talked about that when we discussed resources vs. resourcefulness earlier.

Winning at what Cost?

A topic that occupied centre stage most of 2009-10, and even 2010-11, involves business and personal ethics. In Chapter Four, we discussed the side-effects of winning. We often find winners discarding humility and falling prey to arrogance. The fall of Tiger Woods, Lehman Brothers or the Pakistan cricket team proves that integrity is essential for sustained success. Strong brands like Citibank and Australian cricket exposed the chinks in their armour and disproved their infallibility. It tells us that nothing is permanent and that there is always an opportunity!

Higher work pressures mean that your work-life balance goes for a toss. A leading manager we know well said, 'What is this balance? If you have time from work, then you have a life!' Far too often, one merges into the other. And so, we often joke that the shape of corporate India is characterised by the paunches of its managers. While the West tends to adhere to its five-day week and no-work-at-Christmas policies, Indians, now global managers, seem to work around all time zones. And when they become employers, rather than employees, this could be a potential stress-point. While all business newspapers and magazines write about work-life balance, neither companies nor professionals seem able to walk the talk. The sociological implications of burning the candle from both ends, of pushing oneself beyond one's limits, of sacrificing family life for career are being seen all over. These cannot be good.

Sport teaches us the importance of a healthy mind and body, the value of discipline and work ethic and the need to play not just with others, but also *for* them. The Lone Warrior exists only in fiction. If you have to succeed in today's environment, you need EQ as much as you need IQ. To stay ahead, one first needs to stay relevant. And in a dynamic environment, that means continuous improvement. As Shane Warne commented on Monty Panesar's bowling, 'Is he playing his 33rd Test or is he playing his first Test for the 33rd time?' Innovation has to be an integral part of work culture and we have to constantly strive to do the same things better, more efficiently. Sport shows us that if we combine our ability with the right attitude, and are passionate about our work or business, there is no limit to our advancement. Commit yourself to excellence, and success will definitely follow. Happy winning, to each one of you.

What it Means to be
a Team Player

Even as a child I was drawn to team sport. The fun and friendships shared with teammates, the joy and sorrow of winning or losing together, the ability to get along with others are things familiar to anyone who has played even the most basic level of any team sport. As I graduated to higher levels of cricket and spent a lot of time travelling and playing with teammates, I discovered many more aspects to being a team player.

Apart from enjoying one's own performance, it is highly motivating to participate in the very special process of taking the team to another level. Being in high-pressure situations along with teammates and working towards strategies to counter the opposition can be hugely satisfying, even more so when you actually succeed. Team sport not only provides the space for individual growth but also an opportunity to reach out to those who are not doing that well. And believe me, success is a strangely cyclical phenomenon that all players experience. In any team, there will be people in good form and others who struggle. Very often, then, especially if you are doing well, there is an opportunity to contribute to someone else's success, and experience the pride of seeing your teammate grow as a person. On the other hand, you might be in bad form, but the team still wins, and you have something to be happy about. The beauty of being part of a team is the security it offers along with the realisation that it's not about you alone.

Playing cricket in India means you will have to face the diversity that our country offers. Playing alongside individuals with different abilities and backgrounds teaches you to accept and respect differences without either being intimidated or being snobbish. The dressing room is a place filled with laughter and humour, with everyone pulling each other's leg. But different people have different sensibilities and not everyone can go with the joke to the same extent. When you spend so much time together you learn where to draw the line. You recognise the fine line between laughing with others and laughing *at* others.

Apart from humour, there are so many memories and stories that bind a team together. And winning brings out the best in people, makes them more giving as well as more forgiving. If you notice, all this talk about the great team spirit that defined the Australian team through the late Nineties and early 2000s coincided with their hugely successful run. I am a great believer in the Power of Winning.

I have noticed that good team-players view success very differently from the rest. They are motivated without really worrying about credit. That's not always easy. Anyone who has fielded at short leg knows what a thankless job it is, besides being risky. You put your body on the line, have to work damn hard and may have nothing to show for it. When given that position, there are those who are reluctant to put in the hard work, hoping that they will be made to field in another position the next time round, and there are others who give it their best and actually become specialists.

One can empathise with batsmen who come in to bat at number five, six or seven in a one-day match. They have a limited number of balls to make an impact and show their worth. If they are under pressure to retain their position, they are tempted to take the high-risk option of hitting big shots that may not be in the team's interest at that stage of the match.

Situations like diving or fielding, in which you put your body at risk, or where you are required to play a role outside your core-competence areas, demand more work from a player and therefore require you to put the team ahead of yourself. The funny thing is that you cannot hide your attitude from teammates. If you are selfish, you will be found out in no time at all. But if you are a team-player, the team will know and appreciate that as well.

In his book called *The Sacred Hoops*, Phil Jackson, the legendary coach of the Chicago Bulls, quotes Rudyard Kipling:

For the strength of the Pack is the Wolf and the strength of the Wolf is the Pack.

That, I think, sums it up rather nicely.

—Rahul Dravid

Notes

The Business of Winning

1. Personal interview with authors, September 2010
2. Interview on CNBC-TV18, November 2008
3. In response to e-mail questionnaire
4. In response to e-mail questionnaire
5. Personal interview with authors, September 2010
6. In response to e-mail questionnaire
7. In response to e-mail questionnaire
8. Personal interview with authors, July 2009
9. In response to e-mail questionnaire
10. Interview in *Outlook* magazine, August 2008

Goals

1. Personal interview with authors, July 2009
2. In response to e-mail questionnaire
3. Personal interview with authors, September 2010
4. In response to e-mail questionnaire
5. Interview with *DNA*, June 27, 2010
6. Interview with *The Week in Chess* magazine, sourced from http://www.chess.co.uk/twic/linanand.html
7. In response to e-mail questionnaire

8. Personal interview with authors, July 2009

9. Personal interview with authors, July 2009

The Winning Triangle — Ability, Attitude and Passion

1. Lance Armstrong

2. In response to e-mail questionnaire

3. Martina Navratilova

The Burden of Winning

1. In response to an e-mail questionnaire.

2. Personal interview with authors, July 2009

3. Sourced from http://www.brainyquote.com/quotes/quotes/w/warrenbuff383933

4. Brett Lee

5. Sourced from http://www.brainyquote.com/quotes/quotes/b/billgates122131.html

6. In response to an e-mail questionnaire

7. Sandy Gordon

Learning while Losing

1. Interview by Sujit John and Mini Joseph Tejaswi in *The Times of India,* September 9, 2010

2. Sourced from http://thinkexist.com/quotation/i-ve_missed_more_than-shots_in_my_career-i-ve/216033.html

3. Personal interview with authors, September 2010

4. In response to e-mail questionnaire

5. In response to e-mail questionnaire

6. Personal interview with authors, July 2009

7. Personal interview with authors, July 2009

Change

1. Sourced from http://www.goodreads.com/quotes/show/185636, accessed on 22/3/2011

2. Interview with the *Times of India*, February 24, 2011

3. Sourced from http://thinkexist.com/quotation/he_who_rejects_change_is_the_architect_of_decay/208155.html

4. Personal interview with authors, September 2010

Team Building

1. Personal interview with authors, October 2010

2. Personal interview with authors, May 2010

3. In response to e-mail questionnaire

1. Personal interview with authors, October 2010

2. From *The Independent*, October 14, 2002 sourced from http://www.independent.co.uk/sport/football/international/mccarthy-ecstatic-after-keane-walked-out-613992.html

Leadership

1. Shane Warne

2. Personal interview with authors, May 2010

3. Personal interview with authors, October 2010

4. In response to e-mail questionnaire

5. Personal interview with authors, October 2010

6. In response to e-mail questionnaire

7. In response to e-mail questionnaire

8. In response to e-mail questionnaire

9. Personal interview with authors, July 2009

10. Personal interview with authors, October 2010